Reimagining Religion

A Jesuit Vision

Jim Maher SJ

Published by Messenger Publications, 2023

ISBN: 9781788126083

Designed by Messenger Publications Design Department
Typeset in Adobe Caslon Pro & Adobe Garamond Pro
Printed by Hussar Books

Messenger Publications,
37 Leeson Place, Dublin D02 E5V0
www.messenger.ie

To Fergus Maher RIP
In gratitude

Contents

INTRODUCTION

This book was inspired by a number of challenging conversations about God, spirituality and religion. These conversations had many conclusions. Religion is for the gullible who can't think for themselves. The Bible is contradictory, fanciful and can't be relied upon. Historical details are inaccurate. Religion is for those looking for a security blanket in the face of life's difficulties. It's an insurance policy for the next life, as caustically expressed in W. B. Yeats's poem, 'September 1913', 'For men were born to pray and save.' An intelligent person couldn't possibly accept the dubious claims about God, which are not for enlightened, robust, critical intellectuals who have left such antiquated childish superstitions behind. That was all right in a pre-scientific age when ghouls and goblins ruled the world, and we didn't know any better. When confronted with mysteries we invented supernatural entities, God or the devil. This is humorously highlighted in John B. Keane's play *Sive*, when Nanna recalls the night of Sive's birth. One of the few people in the locality to own a car in the early 1950s was the local doctor. She remembers how the doctor 'came in his new motor car from the village. I remember well to see the two roundy balls of fire coming up the bohareen. The old people swore it was the devil but sure it was only the two headlamps of the car shining in the darkness.'[1] It was a universal phenomenon to resort to imaginary

1.   John B. Keane, *Sive*, Cork: Mercier Press, 2009 (first published 1959), p. 13.

supernatural beings to explain what we couldn't understand. Now that we know better it's essential to reject the idea of God and the naivety of religion as it has nothing to offer except guilt, shame, quirky customs and beliefs, opposing the pleasures of life.

The rejection of Jewish and Christian wisdom, inspired by people's experience of God and refined over centuries of reflection, is like throwing out the baby with the bathwater. The Bible, especially the New Testament, has been the guiding star for millennia, and has served humanity well. We are now at a crossroads. To be or not to be? The planet is suffering, the fragile geopolitical environment is a cause for concern. Choices need to be made. Unless humanity owns its identity there will no longer be a future for our children. The evidence is overwhelming. The lodestar that gave purpose and meaning to life is increasingly a faint flickering light on the brink of extinction, producing in its wake a loss of meaning with all its negative consequences. Biblical wisdom highlights eloquently what it is to be human. We are persons-in-relationship, with God (however we speak about God), others, the planet and ourselves. To be human is to be in relationship. It's hard to find fault with that understanding of the person. We need to reclaim what it is to be human if we want to create a hope-filled future for the generations to come. As experience continually highlights, we reject our identity at our peril. No person is an island, disconnected from interdependence and graced dependence. This is incisively expressed in a powerful image by the poet George Mackay Brown when he writes that 'all that we ever say or think or do – however seemingly unremarkable – may set the whole web of existence trembling and affect the living and the dead and the unborn'.[2] The failure to embrace our identity as persons-in-relationship is the root of all evil.

However, the biblical lodestar has also been abused by biblical fundamentalists, preachers of the prosperity gospel, literalists and others to support their questionable agendas aimed at promoting a self-serving status quo. When authentic religiosity is distorted, it does the opposite of what it's supposed to do; it destroys harmony and undermines peace and solidarity. It becomes a weapon of destruction.

2. Maggie Fergusson, *George Mackay Brown: The Life*, London: John Murray Publishers, 2006, p. 191.

Sadly, the leader of the Russian Orthodox Church used his prestigious position to justify war in Ukraine, a fundamental misunderstanding of Christianity. When unacknowledged cognitive and emotional deficits play a part in decision-making, the only outcome can be flawed decisions and judgements. Individualism, entitlement and exclusion increasingly take precedence over community. Is this what we want for our children? Now is the time to start reigniting the spark of a hope-filled future by reclaiming our identity for the sake of our children before it's too late.

Many people have had Catholic primary and secondary school age-appropriate religious education. On leaving school they went on to employment or to university, with many reaching the pinnacle of their careers. However, their religious literacy was not commensurate with their intellectual development in the other areas of life. Religion was often rejected as its intellectual foundation didn't seem to make any sense. The rejection of religion is often based on a misunderstanding of its intellectual content. Catholic Christianity is often rejected because of its history of abuse. Of course, intense negative feelings also play a part in rejecting childhood faith. Another reason for contemporary rejection lies in the fact that Christianity promotes 'answers to questions no longer being asked, in providing healing for a sickness no longer being acknowledged, and in imparting solace for yearnings stifled by consumption'.[3] In short, Christianity is increasingly perceived as irrelevant, useless and an heirloom from the past. Philip Jenkins, an expert on global Christianity, predicts that Ireland will soon become one of the least religious countries in Europe.[4] In Chapter 1 of *Remnant Christianity*, Trappist monk W. Paul Jones cites study after study that confirm not only the decline of Christianity but also of other world religions; it's a bit like climate change, in that the full brunt of its negative effects will be felt sooner rather than later. In fact, the current loss of meaning experienced by so many, and expressed in destructive ways, is a symptom of our disconnection from our true identity. The graphic images of the destruction of nature as a result of climate change, of the devastation caused by wars

---

3. W. Paul Jones, *Remnant Christianity in a Post-Christian World*, Eugene, OR: Wipf and Stock, 2021. Amazon Kindle edition, p. 306.
4. Ibid., p. 15.

and other evils, is a mirror image of a deep spirit-wound, as the traditional lodestar implodes. What's happening in our world is a spiritual crisis of the most intense magnitude. It's more like a terminal spiritual illness potentially healed by an intense radiation of innate human goodness. The bodily and spiritual inhalation of such ubiquitous toxicity on a daily basis contributes to the destruction of the planet and humanity. There is a small window of opportunity to act now. Procrastination is not an option, in the same way that postponing vaccine research for Covid-19 was not an option. When the challenge of global annihilation became a possibility, all the best scientists rallied to the cause to halt Covid-19 on its destructive path. That same energy and commitment is now required to halt other forms of devastation.

The four Jesuit apostolic preferences are particularly suited to putting us back on track by asking questions about the meaning of life through a process of reflective living. Interpreting our moods helps us to name the unacknowledged 'sickness', otherwise experienced as the influence of our false self, expressing itself through a self-serving culture in which social and climate injustice prevail, and where we're out of touch with the deepest yearnings of the heart. To be human means to wonder, to reach out compassionately to others, and to live our lives in a way that's consistent with the deepest and authentic yearnings of the heart. Being human means expressing our true identity as persons-in-relationship. The history of the world highlights what happens when 'I' and my self-interest supersede the common good, the 'we.'

I would suggest that if common misunderstandings about religion were addressed, they would be redressed. In discussion with frank and honest people, which is always welcome, exhilarating and challenging, it's clear that even before leaving secondary school, at least for many, there was little appetite for developing their religious understanding at a more adult level. It wasn't part of the family ethos or the wider culture. Religion was perceived as backward. Many were Catholic in name only. The death of God would bring liberation from taboos and hang-ups.

The study of theology is not the norm for most people. However, at least a minimum adult exposure to religious literacy is needed to sustain spirituality and religion, especially in a culture where religion is seen as irrelevant and without an intellectual foundation. In a post-modern age, theology, which was once regarded as the queen of science, is no longer held in the same high esteem. Philosophy, the love of wisdom, doesn't enjoy the favour it once did. The advantage of both disciplines is that they teach us how to think in an intelligent way about the meaning of life, even though post-modernism challenges the conclusions of theology and philosophy. We now allow uninformed and unchallenged 'group-think' to do our thinking for us. Radio talk shows are a platform for uninformed people to present opinion as fact. We uncritically and unconsciously give power to media, to the superficial celebrity culture and others to determine our thinking, to dictate fashions and fads, without asking the epistemological and ethical questions. Epistemology deals with how we know, while ethics deals with moral principles, which in a post-modern age, raises its own challenges about how and what we can know.

The purpose of this book, drawing on the apostolic preferences of the Jesuits, is to suggest a way to reimagine the religious and spiritual quest so that it is more relevant to the twenty-first century and can contribute to a hope-filled world for our children. There are four Jesuit apostolic preferences, a technical term for Jesuit works, which are often referred to as apostolates, a term that is derived from the word apostle. The four preferences can be reduced to three, as two of them overlap. The three final chapters of this book will deal specifically with these preferences.

The first apostolic preference suggests putting all life's experience under the reflective microscope, following the guidelines of St Ignatius of Loyola, the founder of the Jesuits, without being obsessively introspective. Regular reflection of this nature will benefit us as it has done countless others. It's not an attempt to convert people to a religion or a spirituality but to broaden perspectives, potentially facilitating human, spiritual and societal development. Reflection, following the guidelines of Ignatius of Loyola, is an interpretive tool to understand our inner life and potentially awaken within us a deeper spiritual awareness that may help us to become more conscious of the mystery we call God. This is what happened to Ignatius, who shared his experience with us. It's not about converting people to a religion. It's about trying to make sense of the conflicting feelings and thoughts that are part of every human life. What can I learn from what I'm feeling and thinking? Spirituality and religion are meant to support us in dealing with life's big questions. 'Why am I here, anyway?' There was a time when I was not. There will be a time when I will no longer be. What's the meaning of the 'in-between'? The Bible is meant to introduce us to God and the life and teachings of Jesus. There's a lot more to God than we think, which resonates with the deepest and truest longings of the heart, if we stop to reflect. However, like the almost extinguished lodestar, God too has got lost along the way, because we bring unexamined, preconceived ideas and unresolved distorted emotions to the biggest question of all. We already bring the answer to the question, that is if we have any interest in the question in the first place. It takes courage to be open to the God-question. Christianity is about liberation from all that destroys life. It's not about condemnation and judgement, unhealthy guilt and shame. It's about freedom from what weighs us down so that we can responsibly live life to the full as individuals and communities. It's about being rescued from our false self to allow our true self to come to the fore. When our false self is in control, we're like a four-engine plane flying on two engines. We're clearly not getting the best deal. The philosopher Socrates spoke about living reflectively. It got him into trouble. It's easier to go with the flow and make no waves. However, without reflection we don't grow. Ignatius of Loyola proposes reflection as a way of life. Learning from experience was essential for him, but applying the learning was even more important. Without reflection there's no way forward. We get stuck in a rut. We get trapped in a rigid worldview both personally and communally, which inspires poor decisions that impact negatively on ourselves and our world. Sooner or later we get stuck in our ways, unable to adapt to change. Ignatius has given us helpful strategies for structured reflection to cover all areas of life. For Ignatius, the Cartesian slogan 'I think, therefore I am' could be better adapted to 'I learn, therefore I am.'[5] Ignatius would agree with Socrates' famous dictum that the 'unexamined life is not worth living', even if the sentiment is a bit extreme – but hyperbole has a way of giving us a jolt. Without regular reflection we get absorbed into our own world and narrow mindset where our limited perceptions become the universal norm.

---

5. Jim Maher, *Pathways To A Decision*, Dublin: Messenger Publications, 2020, p. 69.

We have seen this in various parts of the world where distorted conspiracy theories and fake news are held to be true. One reason they are accepted as truth is that those who believe them are imprisoned by their own fears and unwillingness to reflect and open their minds to consider difficult questions and other points of view. The intensity of negative emotions can be just as damaging as the mistaken beliefs we hold. We need the challenge that serious reflection facilitates. Ignatius of Loyola helps us to sift through our feelings with a view to establishing where they are leading us, to a good or bad space. He also gives us unrivalled guidelines for making good decisions. Even if we're not making decisions, some of the principles can be transferred to various aspects of life to clarify our vision. How often do we make impulsive decisions? How often do we make decisions when we're afraid or angry? How often do we verbally lash out without counting to ten or a hundred, regretting that what was said can never be unsaid, that what we did can never be undone. It's out there for ever, hovering like a ghost coming back to haunt us. If only we had paid heed to good Ignatian advice!

However, it's also important not to let reflective living produce disproportionate worry, anxiety or misguided zeal, as can happen especially to more conscientious and sensitive people. Ignatius's guidelines about interpreting our feelings are helpful in this regard and keep us in a state of emotional and spiritual equilibrium. We may not always be ready for serious reflection as we may find it too daunting. Asking some of the big questions in class one day, a student came to me afterwards admitting that he couldn't deal with such big issues. He found them too unsettling and simply wasn't ready yet for that kind of reflection. In such situations more accessible age-appropriate reflective tools can be helpful. In this context a sense of humour is essential. To be able to laugh is a gift that enables us to put things in perspective and puncture the balloon of our own exaggerated self-importance. Karl Rahner asserts that those who 'cannot admit that not everything is momentous and significant ... [and] always like to be important ... anxious about their dignity' are unable to laugh.[6] Laughter is a way of praising God and it anticipates that God

6.   Harvey D. Egan, *Karl Rahner: Mystic of Everyday Life*, New York, NY: The Crossroad Publishing Company, 1998, p. 125.

will have the last laugh where the sorrows of this world are concerned.[7] Laughter and humour are essential to sustain our lives and prevent us from standing on our dignity. A person thinking of becoming a teacher will need to develop a strong sense of humour to deal with the unfiltered spontaneity of young people. I have been at deathbeds where respectful tears of sadness and laughter complemented one another.

The second and fourth preferences concern social and climate justice. Ignatius's spirituality is pro-active. It's not so much about having private ecstatic spiritual experiences. It's more about letting our lives be formed by ordinary human, spiritual and religious experiences that lead us to a place of compassionate solidarity, a sign that God's life lives within us. The gifts that God blesses us with through life's circumstances are not just for ourselves. Social and climate justice are central to spirituality and religion. For Ignatius spirituality is outward looking. It's the spark that ignites the passion for compassion. Sometimes past students will ask how they can give back for the education they enjoyed so much. Giving back in gratitude for what we have received in life is central to Ignatian spirituality, which is not armchair spirituality. It's about get up and go. Therefore, being concerned about the urgency of social and climate justice in my little patch of the world and further afield in a way that's appropriate to my circumstances is central to religion and spirituality. Thankfully, it appears that 'growing numbers of men and women, including many young people and children, have come to realise that care for creation is an essential expression of our faith'.[8] If this is true, the seeds of a hope-filled future for our children are taking root. One of the most important questions for all of us is, 'How is what I am doing going to impact on the poor and most vulnerable?' This question applies particularly to governments and big business, who have so much power and influence for both good and bad. It is essential for human progress to see the world through the eyes of the poor and most vulnerable, and to have some first-hand experience of what being poor and vulnerable means in its concrete expression.

The third preference concerns accompanying young people in the creation of a hope-filled world. It is significant 'how tragic, how pathetic,

7.   Ibid., pp. 124–6.
8.   Pope Francis, *Vatican News*, 12 February 2022.

is the defining narrative that is emerging of an earth having evolved over billions of years to give birth to the miracle of a self-conscious human-kind who, in turn, through arrogance, greed and fear is bringing itself to the edge of an obliteration that it is apparently incapable of halting'.[9] This stark observation highlights the urgency of creating a hope-filled world in an increasingly unsettled geopolitical environment and a world in which so much damage has been done to Mother Earth. It is possible to create a better world. To think otherwise is a form of despair. I might not be able to change the world, but I can contribute to the creation of a hope-filled world where I live and work. The hardest part is making a start. From there it's the snowball effect. We owe this to the next generation.

It seems difficult to object to these four preferences as the foundation for our spiritual and religious quest. These preferences shape what religion and spirituality could look like in daily life. These four foundations take the focus away from a more traditional pious quest for religion and spirituality, disconnected from social realities and often inspired by fear. They don't represent a 'killjoy' religion or spirituality or any of the dourness and negativity sometimes associated with religion and its traditional obsessions. They represent a worthwhile challenge to make life meaningful. In his beautifully crafted poem, 'The Cure at Troy', Seamus Heaney reminds us that the cultural expectation is not to hope. Yet he suggests that 'once in a lifetime, … justice can rise up / And hope and history rhyme.'[10] This is precisely what the Jesuit preferences are inviting us to do so that God's hope-filled vision for our world can be advanced. No one said it was going to be easy. As the familiar expression states, 'When the going gets tough, the tough get going!' Christians will be a very small group of committed witnesses keeping the flame of faith alive.

To broaden the context and lay the foundation for a discussion of the four preferences, the first two chapters address spirituality and religion, as many people identify themselves as spiritual-without-religion; even if they identify as religious it may be conventional religion-without-spirituality. In the popular mind spirituality and religion seem to be in opposition, which need not be the case. Chapter 3 discusses biblical

9.   W. Paul Jones, op. cit., Amazon Kindle edition, p. 302.
10. Seamus Heaney, *100 Poems*, London: Faber & Faber, 2018, p. 100.

interpretation and how we came to speak about God in the way we do. Misunderstanding the purpose of biblical literature and the important role of literary genre often leads people to reject God and the Bible as fanciful fiction. Two chapters are given over to interpreting the Eucharist, the most important Christian ritual, but one often abandoned by people of faith for complex reasons. There is an attempt to understand it a little better. The verbal imagery of the poet Paul Durcan and the visual imagery of the painter Salvador Dalí cast a helpful light on it.

This book paves the way to a spirituality and religion built on four foundations, reflective living, social and climate justice, and creating a hope-filled world for our young people. These preferences are included in the global identifiers of Jesuit schools. They are challenging. They are meant to influence our values, attitudes and beliefs and lead to action consistent with what it is to be a person-in-relationship. What better legacy could we leave to our children than promoting strategies to support them in enjoying life in a hope-filled world?

Four preferences	Reflection, social/climate justice, hope
Reflection	Pay attention to experience – mull over it – its meaning?
Spiritual	Spirituality starts with awe and wonder.
Lifestyle	Living my identity as a person-in-relationship

CHAPTER 1

I'm Spiritual

'I'm spiritual, but not religious' is a phrase that is often heard. It's often expressed by people doing pilgrimages such as the Camino de Santiago, or climbing Croagh Patrick in County Mayo, or other activities with a traditional spiritual content. It's also expressed in a variety of other contexts and especially when the question of religion is raised. Spiritual but not religious often describes the experience of many people. It's a positive expression because it highlights an awareness of the spiritual dimension that is in everybody's DNA. We all have a spirituality. It's what inspires how we relate to each other, to the planet and to what or who we call God, sometimes referred to as the transcendent, describing what is beyond the range of physical experience.

This was highlighted for me on a Quo Vadis pilgrimage retreat in the Burren with a group of Sixth Years. While we were trekking over rocky, rugged, barren terrain, a French tourist crossed our path. He was amazed to meet twenty young people on an arduous three-day pilgrimage. It challenged his perceptions of young adults. Why would they even think of it? Surely there's more to life for young people than trekking through the lunar-like barren landscape of the Burren? During the conversation that followed, he revealed that he identified himself as spiritual but not religious. He continued by describing how he would visit French churches with their wonderful stained-glass windows and, in the solemn silence, sit there on an upright chair with a simple straw seat. He would be in awe of the church's beauty and workmanship with the smell of residual incense and the smoke of burning candles. He would admiringly take in the details of the rich, colourful stained glass, illuminated by the sunlight, unaware of the passing of time. He revealed that at these moments he felt something deep within, something that took him out of himself into another space that spoke of someone greater than himself, what he described as a glimpse of God, if there is a God. There was a radiant beauty that touched his heart. He felt linked to the generations of believers who had sat there on those same seats, offering up countless prayers of praise, petition, contrition and gratitude, during peacetime and wartime. He would recall those who were baptised, married or nourished by the heavenly manna brought down to earth through the Eucharist. He would recall those carrying heavy burdens finding solace in the confessional. He would wistfully imagine those being shouldered down the aisle by family members and friends on their journey to their final resting place. This building was more than bricks and mortar, a place where an image of a broken body nailed to a crucifix hung above the altar. This was indeed sacred space, which accommodated saints and sinners, hope and despair, hurt and healing, faith and doubt. He longed to be able to embrace his ancestral faith. He was seriously engaging with the spiritual dimension of his life.

'I'm not religious,' he reminded us again, 'but I am spiritual.' He concluded that he had a similar experience when listening to the sound of the majestic organs that filled the large, cavernous spaces of some of France's great cathedrals. 'You're a seeker,' I humbly and tentatively suggested in response to such mysticism, an apprehension of an experience not easily understood. He agreed, saying that that's exactly how he would identify himself, like so many others, a searching spiritual person. It was as if someone or something was tugging at his heartstrings, stirring an existential restlessness that translated into a quest. Perhaps it was God directly touching his spirit through his aesthetic sensibility, knowing full well that that was the way to knock on the door of his sensitive and intuitive nature. God makes use of our gifts of personality to enter our hearts. The door to our Frenchman's heart was his aesthetic sensibility and sensitivity to the possibility of a God. He hadn't yet realised who was knocking. Perhaps he would some day, or maybe such spirituality-without-religion would be his manna for the rest of his days. The result of his spiritual experiences was always positive, underpinning a responsible and altruistic lifestyle, a clear sign, Ignatius of Loyola would say, that God was at work. In his 'spiritual exercises' Ignatius gives us helpful guidelines to interpret our 'spiritual' experiences.

Our Frenchman's experience is not unique. Many of us who don't call ourselves religious recognise experiences where we feel drawn out of ourselves. Existential restlessness is part of us all, as it concerns the most important questions in life: 'What am I doing here, anyway? What's my life about? What happens when I die?' They are not usually the questions we ask when getting out of bed in the morning. We have more urgent matters to attend to, getting the kids off to school, preparing the lunch boxes, arguing with the teenage son preening himself in the bathroom while the queue is gathering outside the door. However, what we do during the day reveals the answer to our big-ticket questions, at least partially. Spirituality inspires how we live, especially what we do, and how we spend our time. The word 'spirituality' owes its origin to the Latin word '*spiritus*', which has connotations of life-giving breath. We could perhaps call it by another name, such as our value system and beliefs. If I spend the day with a compassionate attitude matched by compassionate actions, I have a spirituality that's inspired by something good and life-giving, leading me towards a space that enriches me as a human being. If I spend my day demeaning and exploiting others, I have a 'spirituality' that is life-denying and is undermining my humanity, because the fundamental human orientation is to live life, not undermine it.

Spirituality is usually understood in a positive sense. Spirituality is what inspires what's good as we inhale life-giving breath that transforms us for the better. Many are inspired to do good, but equally many are inspired to do what's not good. What's not good presents itself to us under the guise of good. That's why we're attracted to it. What seem like innocent shortcuts in business, disguised as good, can eventually lead to a troubling space. Political dictators and others who destroy people's lives operate out of a misguided spirituality. The proof of this can be found in where their actions lead. The Russian invasion of Ukraine, with scant regard for life and the rule of law, is a graphic and terrifying image of death and destruction. The destruction of innocent human life is totally unacceptable. On the other hand, the mayhem started by Putin drew out the best in countless people who supported those displaced and devastated. The core of a positive spirituality nourished by the good habits of a lifetime came to the fore. The criterion for distinguishing an authentic spirituality from an inauthentic one is how life-giving the spirituality is. St Ignatius of Loyola develops this idea through the metaphor of a good spirit and a bad spirit. He suggests that the good spirit is a peace-giver who builds up individuals and communities. The bad spirit does the opposite and comes from a dark place. It comes from the fear, anger, insecurity, entitlement, inferiority, delusions and narcissism that drive destructive behaviour. The bad spirit is better referred to as the enemy of our human nature, while the good spirit is the friend of our human nature. In biblical imagery the enemy of our human nature is called Satan. Sadly, when negative spirits are doing the driving, we're likely to harm ourselves and our communities, as the Russian invasion of Ukraine vividly demonstrates. Conspiracy theories have a similar effect. In the US they stirred up fear and insecurity, attacking rational and reflective discourse, which culminated in the attack on the Capitol that undermined democracy and the rule of law. Half-truths, fake news, 'alternative facts' and intense prejudices become the Truth. The bad spirit – the enemy of our human nature – is destructive, alienating and dehumanising. Therefore, Ignatius concludes that we need to practise regular reflection to determine whether we're being inspired by a good spirit or a bad spirit (which need not be interpreted literally as spiritual beings). He gives us helpful guidelines to help us to make good judgements about the origin of our inspirations and, in particular, to pay attention to where they're leading. This activity is technically known as 'the discernment of spirits'. He also gives invaluable wisdom on how to make good decisions. He stresses the need to be aware of the negative feelings that can drive our behaviour. Ignatian reflection is an invaluable tool for personal and societal growth. To understand where we're coming from is half the battle in getting where we want to go.

Within the human heart there are always going to be contradictory stirrings. Therefore, we need to pay attention to what's authentic and to what's preventing us from growing into an integrated and balanced human person. 'I'm spiritual' – but, as we have seen, not all spirituality is equal. Inspiration can be both good and bad. There is compelling evidence that contemporary society has lost its way. This is confirmed by daily news bulletins. Community is replaced by individualism, exaggerated nationalism, xenophobia, exploitation, human trafficking, wars, famine, conspiracy theories and other events that contradict community and graced dependence – all clear symptoms of death, dehumanisation and alienation destroying life. It's clear that the enemy of our human nature is at work. Humans are responsible for much of the evil in the world. Man's inhumanity to man is a constant theme. The effects of war do not happen by chance. Poverty and homelessness don't happen by chance. There is human agency somewhere along the line. Greed, materialism, big egos, fears, insecurities, entitlement and prejudices are often the driving forces. Therefore, the importance of regular reflection to assess which direction we're moving in, personally and collectively, cannot be emphasised enough. Ignatius gives us a short daily exercise called the 'examen' to help us in this process. It's a prayerful, reflective exercise focusing on what we have received and how we respond. But it also helps us to uncover motivation for patterns in our lives that we're not proud of, what is traditionally called sin. This exercise proposed by the first Jesuit apostolic preference is a valuable tool for more reflective living.

Human beings desire happiness. We sometimes look for it in the wrong places and end up unhappier than when we went on our quest for happiness in the first place. Sometimes it's this unreflective choice that spawns further personal and communal unhappiness. That recreational drug won't do me any harm. It's only a bit of fun. I'm okay, I'll drive. Human experience confirms that we're happiest when we're exercising compassion and generosity in the variety of ordinary circumstances of life, through all those 'little, nameless, unremembered, acts / Of kindness and of love' (William Wordsworth, 'Tintern Abbey') that usually fill most of our day. Attentiveness to others establishes a contentment and peace, that strengthens us to welcome joys and embrace the burdens of sorrow. Irresponsible stimuli sometimes pass for happiness. However, they are usually superficial and transitory, leaving a hollow afterglow. Happiness is the peace and contentment that helps us to stay the course responsibly. Superficial feelings of elation pass quickly. Developing a healthy spirituality will help us to find a lasting peace because the path to peace comes from reflective living and learning from experience what it really is to be an authentic person. If there is no pattern of at least some minimal reflection, we're living shallow lives. The tradition of confession in the Christian tradition was meant to be an opportunity for some self-reflection to acknowledge our failings while welcoming God's mercy in the light of God's desire for our true self to blossom, but for many it became a laundry list of rules that had been broken. Confession was based on an act-centred morality that failed to grasp the complexity of a person's life. Then the focus changed after the Second Vatican Council, when confession required 'in the penitent the will to open his heart to the minister of God'.[11] This marks a shift from act-centred morality to a more holistic conversation that acknowledges the fullness of the person. The principles of Ignatian reflection can be a support in preparing for this conversation, which for many is not easy. There are still those whose experience of this sacrament is unhelpful.

A characteristic of a spiritual person is the humility to allow for the possibility that there is more to life than meets the eye. It's the capacity to distinguish between appearances and reality. This is well-expressed in Shakespeare's *Hamlet*, when the Prince of Denmark says to his friend Horatio that 'There are more things in heaven and earth, Horatio, / Than are dreamt of in your philosophy.'[12] Hamlet is making the point that the physical world we inhabit is unable to explain everything there is to be explained. There are many who call themselves unbelievers because God cannot be proved or disproved like scientific facts or a mathematical formula, or because they reject an image of God that believers also reject. If Hamlet is right, then it's not possible to reject the existence of God unless we understand everything there is to be understood. Who can say they understand everything that's to be understood? Even if we did understand everything there is to be understood, another question arises: 'Why is there anything to be understood in the first instance anyway?' It seems presumptuous to reject God's existence when we have such finite minds. It seems more honest to remain at least open-minded until such time as we have compelling evidence to assert that God definitely does not exist. Referring to Job, Agur (Proverbs, chapter 30) and Ecclesiastes, Abraham Heschel makes the point that 'what stirred their souls was neither the hidden nor the apparent, but the hidden in the apparent; not the

---

11. Bishops' Committee on the Liturgy U.S.A., *Rite of Penance*, New York, NY: Catholic Book Publishing Co., 1976), p. 12.
12. Act 1, Scene 5.

order but the mystery of the order that prevails in the universe. We live on the fringe of reality and hardly know how to reach the core.'[13]

Our lived experience is only the tip of an iceberg. There is so much we really don't know about ourselves, our planet and the galaxies. For all we know there may be a more advanced civilisation elsewhere. It's an open question. The possibility cannot be ruled out at this stage. We don't know enough about space. If the day comes when we discover life elsewhere, what will it mean for us? No one knows. There are many medical conditions we still don't know how to cure, at least for the time being. While there's so much we don't know and will never know in our lifetime, some of us are certain beyond any doubt that there couldn't be any kind of entity we call God. It's helpful to review the steps that lead us to such a conclusion, given the magnitude of such an assertion and its implications.

In Celtic spirituality there are 'thin places'. Such numinous environments are places where there is a sense of a thin veil between the material and spiritual. The fact remains that the 'world is something we apprehend but cannot comprehend'.[14] We comprehend some of our apprehensions, but not all. Thin places can facilitate an intuitive experience that senses a divine, otherworldly, transcendent presence, which raises questions about our experience of human limitation and why there is something rather than nothing. For many, such an experience can take place in rugged landscapes or beautiful seascapes or when a baby is born. Many people share their experience of such a common phenomenon. Is it subjective? Or is there more to it? Can spirituality bring this experience to a level of understanding?

The idea of a global 'thin place' is echoed in Pope Francis's *Laudato Si'*: 'The entire material universe speaks of God's love and boundless affection for us. Soil, water, mountains: everything is a caress of God.'[15] Spirituality is learning how to detect the caress of that ultimate reality and how to respond to that caress in a way that enriches our experience of life and contributes to the care of our common home and those

13. Abraham Joshua Heschel, *God in Search of Man: A Philosophy of Judaism*, New York, NY: Farrar, Strauss & Giroux, 1976. Amazon Kindle edition, p. 56.
14. Ibid., p. 58.
15. Pope Francis, *Laudato Si'* (On Care for Our Common Home), Dublin: Veritas Publications, 2015, par. 84.

with whom we share it. One way to acknowledge the 'caress of God' is to remember the enigmatic words of the poet Keats when he writes in 'Ode on a Grecian Urn', 'Beauty is truth, truth beauty, – that is all / Ye know on earth, and all ye need to know.' Does our experience of beauty in its many forms draw us beyond the commonplace to an intuition of a transcendent truth that is beyond full comprehension? It's not exactly clear what Keats is conveying. However, the final lines of the poem are hauntingly provocative, suggesting the possibility that beauty lifts us up beyond ourselves to intuit something of God, the fullness of truth and beauty. Perhaps this is the kind of experience our Frenchman was having in the great French cathedrals, similar to Wordsworth when he writes: 'With an eye made quiet by the power / of harmony, and the deep power of joy / We see into the life of things' ('Tintern Abbey'). Our experience of beauty – welcoming new life into the world, awe at a sunset, listening to music, watching a good film or accompanying a vulnerable person, has the capacity to crack the shell of self-absorption so that we look upwards and outwards with the eye of the heart. Dostoevsky got it right in *The Idiot* when he suggested that the world is saved by beauty. Whatever lifts us out of our own enclosed personal universe deserves to be called our 'saviour'. The beauty of relationships and beauty in so many other guises crack open our thick, protective shells.

However, millions on our planet do not experience the optimistic spirituality expressed through the imagery of God's caress because the health of the planet has been undermined. To find God's caress in the bleakness of a famine-ridden, hopeless, arid landscape is a mammoth task. While humans throughout history have been heroic and self-sacrificing, inspired by a life-enriching spirituality, the opposite is also true. Philip Larkin expresses this well when he writes in the final stanza of 'This Be The Verse', 'Man hands misery on to man / It deepens like a coastal shelf.'[16] The point about passing a toxic mix from one generation to the next, albeit unintentionally, is well made. That's one of the reasons why reflection on our spirituality is so critical. In Christian terminology this toxicity is called 'original sin.' Other more helpful terms may also express this reality. What kind of spirituality

16. Philip Larkin, *High Windows*, London: Faber & Faber, 2015, p. 25.

do I hand on to my children, especially in the context of accompanying young people in the creation of a hope-filled world? Larkin certainly rattles the cage in this poem, especially in his hyperbolic and robust opening lines, highlighting how parental fault-lines can be unintentionally passed on to our own children when he writes: 'They fuck you up, your mum and dad. / They may not mean to, but they do. / They fill you with the faults they had / And add some extra, just for you.'[17] Experience also suggests that we tend to break everything – hearts, promises, relationships, solidarity, the planet, one another, political treaties – anything, in fact, that we can get our hands on. We get fed up, go in search of illusory better stimuli and come to grief. We can't stay the course. We need to be anywhere but where we are. We're asking, 'Are we there yet?', the 'there' in question being some non-existent fantasy land. Anything to escape reality! And we're good at finding excuses to justify our breakages. It's always much easier to blame someone else for our actions. We've been doing it since Adam first blamed Eve, who blamed the serpent, for taking the fruit from the tree of knowledge. A reflective spirituality inspires us to learn from our mistakes so that we can mend what's broken and prevent future breakages. St Ignatius's stress on the necessity for reflection is one of his greatest legacies. If I'm not learning from my experience of life, I'm going nowhere fast. I'm simply going round in circles on a carousel.

The writer Antoine de Saint-Exupéry has given us a helpful idea to challenge our perspectives. His novella *The Little Prince* shares a secret with us, 'a very simple secret: It is only with the heart that one can see rightly; what is essential is invisible to the eye … the eyes are blind. One must look with the heart.'[18] A spiritual person often develops a sensitivity to what's not obvious to others. Another Frenchman, Blaise Pascal, reminds us that 'The heart has its reasons, which reason knows nothing of … We know truth not only by reason, but by heart.' Spirituality involves both reason, emotion and the intuition that comes from them.

17. Ibid.
18. Antoine de Saint-Exupéry, *The Little Prince*, London: William Heinemann, 1945; 1991 edition (London: Mammoth), p. 68.

Knowledge, therefore, is both head and heart. This was beautifully illustrated by Vincent Van Gogh in a tender black chalk and pencil image called *Girl Kneeling in Front of a Cradle*. He writes to his brother Theo, 'But if one feels the need of something grand, something infinite, something that makes one feel aware of God, one need not go far to find it. I think I see something deeper, more infinite, more eternal than the ocean in the expression of the eyes of a little baby when it wakes in the morning, and coos or laughs because it sees the sun shining on its cradle. If there is a "ray from on high," perhaps one can find it there.'[19] This is a concrete expression of Saint-Exupéry's 'What's essential is invisible to the eye.' It's the kind of experience we all have from time to time. However, it may evade us if we're not reflective.

Van Gogh articulates what many of us experience at the arrival of new life. Even the most hard-hearted are moved at the sight of a healthy newborn baby, which has the potential to inspire humility in the face of all our questions and uncertainties about ultimate reality. In the ultrasound clinic, expectant mothers wait anxiously with their partners. When they receive good news, they treasure the image of developing life presented by the radiologist and their whole demeanour changes. Once they get home, they share the image and their joy with family and friends, feeling as if they are part of a miraculous event. They are filled with gratitude for the wonderful blessing they have received. Their first instinct is often to give thanks to God or a higher power, without ignoring their self-sacrifice in facilitating a safe delivery.

Like parents, those who work with animals often never cease to marvel at the miracle of birth. Vets and farmers often go out of their way to save life, not always motivated by economic reasons. In the middle of a blizzard, farmers will go out into the darkness of night to help their ewes in labour. A spiritual dynamic is at work. There is huge respect as the mystery of new life unfolds. Such a way of looking at things reinforces the idea that what is essential is invisible to the eye. A new birth is indeed a 'ray from on high', a hint that there is more to life than appearances. Appearances in whatever shape or form are reflections of another reality.

19. Cliff Edwards, *Van Gogh and God: A Creative Spiritual Quest*, Chicago, IL: Loyola University Press, 1989, p. 160.

As we watch the sun rise in the East and set in the West, day in, day out, we are witnessing a daily miracle. If the sun were to set only once in the whole of history, it would be regarded as a miracle and would generate awe and wonder, but the miracle of a daily sunset loses its lustre, just like everything else we get used to. Many have lost the capacity to dwell in a 'wonder-space', which originates from a reflective lifestyle where we pay attention. This is highlighted in the Oscar-nominated film, *The Hand of God*, from the Italian director Paulo Sorrentino. Writing about this film critic José Solis remarks that Sorrentino 'has created some of the modern cinema's most breath-taking imagery, often finding beauty in the mundane, a reminder of how we should realise just how many miracles occur around us daily – if only we bothered to look.' He then quotes Sorrentino, who asserts that 'Being in touch with the divine is a deep need that cannot be suppressed for mankind as a whole.' Solis also makes the point that the divine 'can find us through the most unexpected of sources.'[20] And perhaps the gift of so much beauty, if we have the eyes to see, gets us to connect with its creator, who has our best interests at heart even when we don't see it that way.

Sadly, it may not always be beauty that opens our eyes to the wonder of the world and triggers questions about ultimate reality. Many of us have had family tragedies and bereavements that cause deep wounds in the core of the heart that never fully heal. The heart remains broken. It doesn't take much for the wound to open – anniversaries, birthdays and Christmas. In the past there were neat theories about the grieving process that didn't resonate with experience. Those who have suffered bereavements and tragedies know that the challenge is to live with a wound that will never fully heal. Grief is not something we can walk around. We have to make our way through eye of the storm until we come out on the other side. We can't will our pain away. However, such painful experiences can eventually raise questions about the meaning and purpose of life, but only when we're ready to embrace them. The sudden death of a person is like stopping a conversation in mid-sentence, especially where there is much left unsaid. The illness and death of a child is incomprehensible, as are so many other premature deaths. Death in all

20. *National Catholic Reporter*, 12 March 2022.

its horror challenges our understanding of what life is about. It's a good argument for suggesting that God does not exist, that God, if there is a God, is capricious, and that life is meaningless.

Robert Frost wonders along these lines in the final couplet of 'Design', a short poem recalling the death of a moth captured by a spider on a white flower, which should normally be blue. He asks, 'What but design of darkness to appal?– / If design govern in a thing so small.' This provocative poem indirectly raises questions about what kind of God there is, and the interplay between God as the designer of an ordered world and random destructiveness – these are complex scientific questions giving rise to philosophical and theological reflection.

However, suffering is an experience which we cannot fully understand. W. B. Yeats expresses it well in his poem 'The Stolen Child', when addressing a child about to leave this world for an enchanted 'faery' land to escape the pain of lost innocence. He asserts that 'the world's more full of weeping than you can understand'. While there's some suffering over which we have no control, we can also play a part in the creation of suffering through deliberate irresponsibility, which impacts negatively on others and our planet, and which gives rise to another question. Why do we make such poor choices that can cause misery? If Ignatian reflection were to be applied to our decisions, we would make fewer uninformed and dysfunctional emotive decisions. In the face of suffering, countless people have found a way forward with the support of spirituality, religion, family and friends, which emphasises the need for the empathetic solidarity that so many are good at. One of the greatest theologians of the twentieth century, German Jesuit Karl Rahner, when 'challenged by an interviewer because of his great faith despite the horrors of Nazism', said, 'I believe because I pray.'[21] It's quite significant that such a brilliant theologian, who wrote about the most complex and perplexing theological questions, which don't lend themselves to easy solutions, could make such an enigmatic and challenging statement. I don't believe he meant only saying prayers by rote. Prayerful attention to experience has the power to unlatch the gate to belief, experienced at first somewhere in the depths of the heart, those inklings of someone greater than us, which in turn lead to a quest for understanding our inklings. It's that hint of the

21. Harvey D. Egan, op. cit., p. 81.

mysterious Other, experienced in prayerful and reflective wonder, which has the potential to ignite the spark of belief. In the context of Rahner's interview, the Christian tradition asserts that suffering does not have the final say and that we're accompanied by the crucified one as a fellow combatant in the face of suffering of every kind. However, without reflective living, faith is less likely to germinate.

Tolstoy wrote about his experience of looking into the coffin of his deceased mother, whom he lost as a boy. He describes how for 'a time I lost all sense of existence and experienced a kind of vague blissfulness which, though grand and sweet, was also sad. It may be that, as it ascended to a better world, her beautiful soul had looked down with longing at the world ... that it had seen my sorrow, and pitying me, had returned to earth on the wings of love to console and bless me with a heavenly smile of compassion.'[22] He describes mixed feelings. But the 'blissfulness' he speaks about doesn't come for many of us until a long time afterwards, if at all. For many it's the experience of lingering sadness, which is appreciated only by those who have been through the experience. It's impossible for those who haven't had the first-hand experience to appreciate the intensity and complexity of grief. On the other hand, that experience of being with his mother seems to have been a moment of reassurance for Tolstoy. What he describes sounds like an intuitive apprehension of another reality, which is intrinsic to spirituality. Christianity especially doesn't play down the suffering of the world and doesn't have glib answers, but it situates it in a more hopeful context that doesn't diminish the intensity of grief, pain and unanswered questions. This may become a little clearer in the chapters on Mass. Getting our heads around death really puts us to the pin of our collar. Our hope is that we can discover a spirituality that helps us to manage this question and gives us direction.

One of the most striking and moving Pietà sculptures is located in Lisbon Cathedral. The dead Jesus is on his mother's lap. Her tear-filled eyes are looking away from him out into the middle distance as if she's in despair, looking for a glimmer of hope. Is she having her 'My God, my God, why have you abandoned me?' moment, as her son had while

22. Leo Tolstoy, 'Childhood', Classic Bookshelf (website), www.classicbookshelf.com/library/leo_tolstoy/childhood/26/.

he was dying? Is her faith being tested? I suspect that she was having that moment of desperation in response to her disintegrating world. More than likely, she was numb from shock, taking in little or nothing, and, like any other mother, was struggling with the prospect of her son's funeral. Sometimes the piety surrounding Mary dilutes the fact that she was human and capable of doubt like the rest of us. She had just seen out of the world her cherished son whom she so lovingly brought into the world, nurtured, nourished, doted over and made into the man he was. Experience seems to confirm that the relationship between a mother and son is special. Jesus could not have been so compassionate if his mother and father had not convincingly modelled the spirituality of compassion at home. Like the rest of us, Mary had a choice. Do I embrace what's happened as best as possible or do I allow it to overwhelm me? A difficult and painful question, because Christian faith doesn't work like a magic wand. The capacity to accept suffering doesn't come in the twinkling of an eye, and all the pious but well-meaning platitudes do not make matters any better. It's like saying to a depressed person, 'Get a grip on yourself, cheer up, there's many who are worse off than you!' But Mary's spirit was not to be defeated. Underlying her spirituality, at the core of her heart, was her fundamental conviction, rooted in her Jewish religious experience, that God could be trusted even in the darkest hours. It's a bit like going through severe pain, under the guidance of trusted doctors, in the knowledge that we'll come out the other side pain-free. The pain and the trust coexist. Like the rest of us, in the spirit of Gerard Manley Hopkins's poem 'The Wreck of the Deutschland', at that particular period of her life Mary had not yet had that 'Let him easter in us' moment for which we often have to wait patiently in the darkness until there is 'a dayspring to the dimness of us' when we're ready to accept it, and which doesn't always come easily. In any event, when Mary held her dead son, there was at that time no resurrection in the sense in which we have come to understand it. Therefore, she was in the dark, with nothing but trust in God, which was rewarded.

It's helpful to linger by meditatively considering works of art that touch the heart. However, many of us have an attention deficit because we flit from one stimulus to another in pursuit of more. Observe tourists in the Louvre. They reach the *Mona Lisa*. After a few seconds they tick it off their bucket list after the selfie, which is not allowed. Admittedly, it is difficult to enjoy the *Mona Lisa* while crowds jostle for position. This constant quest for novel stimulation undermines spirituality, religion and life. The image of people waiting at a bus stop engaging with their phones represents this phenomenon. This issue is addressed by philosopher Byung-Chul Han in his book *The Disappearance of Rituals*, where he remarks that there is an 'intensification of serial perception. Perception is never at rest: it has lost the capacity to linger … The cultural technique of deep attention emerged precisely out of ritual and religious practices. It is no accident that "religion" is derived from *relegere*: to take note. Every religious practice is an exercise in attention.'[23] He translates '*relegere*' as 'taking note' but it also expresses the related idea of 'rereading'. When we reread something, we are immersing ourselves in the experience. We're not reading for stimulation or knowledge. We know what we have already read. In his spiritual quest our Frenchman was not looking for stimulation or knowledge. He was lingering in sacred space. When we reread (*relegere*) or immerse ourselves in nature, music, a work of art or a spiritual and religious ritual, we are creating a special space where our heart is touched. It's not surprising that many choose to walk on their favourite beach or forest track to switch off the overactive craving for stimulation and enter that silent space where we're focused on this moment without expecting stimulation or new perception. It's a difficult space to linger in because of our cultural conditioning where we become slaves to serial perception. That 'taking note' Han speaks about, that paying attention to, is a bit like a mother's attention to her child as the child begins to sleep. The mother is simply present to the child in the moment with no other agenda. Religious rituals are a bit like that. They are anchors in the streams of life to moor us and to buoy us up in a personal place where we can reread who we are. Han suggests that attention deficit owes its origin to the inability to simply be and pay attention. Paying attention is a prerequisite for prayer and ritual; it's not surprising that prayerful people are resilient because they draw something precious from

23. Byung-Chul Han and Daniel Steuer, *The Disappearance of Rituals: A Topology of the Present*, Cambridge: Polity Press, 2020. Amazon Kindle edition, p. 7.

the wells of their contemplative experience which influences the way they experience the world and their capacity to recognise that 'what's essential is invisible to the eye'.[24]

Some Camino pilgrims continue to Finisterre (the end of the world) in Galicia, another three days' hike. They sit in silence in a quiet nook on the cape overlooking the Atlantic Ocean. In their quiet reflective space, somewhat like lingering quietly in a great cathedral, they take in the wonder and magnificence of the scenery with the ocean stretching far to the horizon and the roaring sound of the sea below. It's a 'thin place', whose awesomeness cannot but touch hearts. Many return to their routine activities with an altered perspective for the better, a sure sign that God is present, even if it's not articulated that way. Lingering spiritually in sacred space helps to humanise us and helps us to reconnect with our true self. These lingerings are often not recognised as experiences of God because our image of God is not calibrated to acknowledge God's presence in ordinary events. Many of us would be too embarrassed or lack the vocabulary to speak of such personal sacred moments.

While acquiring scientific knowledge about our planet is vitally important, the more personal affective impact as we watch a sunrise or sunset or any other powerful natural event is equally important. How do they impact our spirit? What do such events inspire in us? Wonder? Feeling part of something bigger than ourselves? It's like the difference between prose and poetry. Prose is deliberately logical and rational, while poetry impacts the spirit and facilitates acknowledgement of feelings, sometimes in a way that's hard to put into words. Life is full of those 'hard to put into words' moments, whether it's the experience of sexual intimacy, powerful soulful music, arriving at Santiago de Compostela after a long arduous pilgrimage (beautifully illustrated in the closing shots of the film *The Way*), or listening to the haunting Taizé chants in the semi-darkness of a candle-lit church accompanied by people from all over the world. It could be the sound of a gushing waterfall against the backdrop of majestic mountains. It could be a baby's first words. It's one of those special beautiful moments that takes us beyond ourselves, a moment where we savour the moment.

24. Antoine de St-Exupéry, op. cit.

Seeing the world with childlike wonder triggers spirituality. But wonder can quickly be beaten out of us. One day in a supermarket, a frustrated mother was wheeling her child in the trolley while shopping. The child kept asking questions, as children do. It's natural for toddlers looking out through their eyes at the world for the first time to question incessantly. It's a sign of normality and an expression of wonder at new experiences. Why has that man no hair on his head, mummy? What's that on the woman's ears, mummy? Why is the dog barking? It can go on and on as it did in this case. By the time the frustrated mother had come to the check-out, the child was told in no uncertain terms, expressed in inappropriate language, to be quiet.

If such is the common experience of a child when they express wonder-questions, they will lose the capacity for wonder because they learn that asking certain questions only irritates adults. They appropriate the dictum that 'children should be seen and not heard'. Jewish theologian Abraham Heschel rightly remarks that the 'reason why the adult no longer wonders is not because he has solved the riddle of life, but because he has grown accustomed to the laws governing his world picture … and he who has reached the stage where he no longer wonders about anything, merely demonstrates that he has lost the art of reflective reasoning'.[25] When we lose the art of reflective reasoning, the foundations of spirituality and religion begin to crumble, because we then take things for granted, which, in turn, intensifies our sense of entitlement.

As enquiring children develop, they may ask fewer questions. In classrooms, peer pressure can often prevent other students from asking questions for fear of being ridiculed. Wonder is an essential life attitude, not just for spirituality but for so many other aspects of life, such as science. Without wonder there is no spirituality, no scientific enquiry, no philosophy, no theology and no literature or art. The spiritual person takes seriously the idea of the philosopher Socrates that the unexamined life is not worth living. Too often, the unexamined assumptions many of us take for granted prop up structural injustice and a stale, unimaginative status quo where structures that don't work are reinforced. It's often easier to go with the flow, supporting the status quo. Spirituality helps to unmask the untruths that are accepted as truths by conventional wisdom. This is

25. Abraham Joshua Heschel, op. cit., Amazon Kindle edition, pp. 51–52.

what Socrates was trying to do. He was challenging people to think for themselves and ask the right questions, at a time, like the present, when many are happy to let others do their thinking for them. It's not difficult to work out where groupthink leads to. We can take ways of thinking for granted, in the same way that we take our material stuff for granted. The role of responsible and intelligent reflection cannot be overemphasised.

Paying attention to ordinary life experience is also the foundation of spirituality. A former hunting lodge on the slopes of a mountain once accommodated a group of students on retreat. When darkness came, the interior lights, run on gas, had to be individually lit, giving a faint glimmer of illumination and creating a cosy atmosphere for the students sitting before a blazing log fire. When the retreat activities were finished for the evening, the young people were invited to take a short walk away from the lodge to look up at the stars on a cloud-free night, miles away from the interference of any electrical light. The response was remarkable. There was a palpable experience of wonder and awe at such an incredible sight. Reflective space is essential for the spiritual spark to glow. With so many living such pressurised lives, with the immediate and the urgent claiming priority, it can be challenging to create even minimal reflective wonder-space. Busy family life can make reflection a luxury beyond the capacity of overburdened parents working every hour that God sends to put bread on the table and a roof over the family's heads. However, it's not impossible, and it may even help us to manage the stresses of the day in a more creative way. Serial perception and constant stimuli are not good for the spirit. The spirit needs unpressurised space to recollect so that we recover our humanity.

Spirituality has the potential to focus our perspective and to widen our horizons so that we experience more peace and contentment. Spirituality can help us to question and enrich the way we live and unearth faulty expectations that stress us out. Is it right that economic forces dictate our lifestyle to the extent that we are dispensable cogs in an economic machine controlled by impersonal others who dump us as soon as we're surplus to requirements? Or that workers will be fired at the drop of a hat to make way for agency workers who are cheaper to employ, or that long-serving employees will be made redundant to accommodate employees on cheaper rates? Just as the sabbath was made for humankind and not humankind for the sabbath, so too economic systems must be there to serve humankind rather than enslave it. Spirituality can help us to contextualise our lives. It helps us to form good relationships between ourselves and the wider community, the planet, the person we call God. Spirituality isn't an added extra on the menu of life. It's essential to who we are so that we can successfully negotiate life. It's the glue that holds everything together. It's not surprising that a person with an explicit spirituality tends to be more resilient in the face of life's difficulties. In the inevitable storms of life, a haven is essential so that we can take stock and reset our course. Spirituality won't get rid of the storms of life, but, like a life jacket, it will help to keep us afloat. It won't take away the pain, the sorrow, disappointment and failure that inevitably come our way, but it will give us perspective that will help us to carry on.

American poet Gregory Orr had his own personal tragedies to deal with. At twelve years of age, he accidentally killed his brother with a hunting rifle. Two years later his mother died. His father's temperament made family circumstances difficult. Gregory was unlawfully arrested as a teenager and unjustly beaten up by police for taking part in a demonstration supporting the Black civil rights movement and was kidnapped at gunpoint. He expresses his belief 'in poetry as a way of surviving the emotional chaos, spiritual confusions and traumatic events that come with being alive'.[26] When he found his vocation as a poet, he found his way forward in life. Perhaps we could say something similar for spirituality. We need the light of an inspiring spirituality that helps us to get out of bed in the morning, enabling us to laugh and have a sense of humour, sustaining us as we cope with sorrows, failure and disappointment while celebrating the joys of life. Those inevitable moments of being able to intuit and see with the heart are momentary flashes of enlightenment and beauty highlighting a 'divine caress'. Are we open-minded enough to pay attention with the eye of the heart? Or has routine undermined

---

26. Gregory Orr, 'The Making of Poems', NPR (website), https://www.npr.org/2006/02/20/5221496/the-making-of-poems.

our sense of wonder? Ultimately, our spirituality is what inspires our lifestyle, attitudes, values and beliefs. If we pay attention to how we live, we'll connect with what's really driving us. Are we being driven towards what's life-giving or life-denying? That's the foundational question for our spirituality.

Spirituality	Reflection – why – what?
Meaning	Values – attitudes – beliefs
Why something – not nothing?	A higher power – a god?
Lifestyle	Lifestyle expresses spirituality.
My spirituality	Life-enhancing – life-denying

CHAPTER 2

I'm Not Religious

Is there really a difference between spirituality and religion? Could my spirituality be my religion and vice versa? Spirituality implies everything outlined in Chapter 1. However, being spiritual-without-religion suggests a private experience, cut off from a shared spirituality that is communally expressed. The focus tends to be on my spiritual experience. It's what I'm working out for myself by myself. I may have a mix-and-match from different philosophical or religious traditions without any engagement with a community. Spirituality is based on my personal experience, which is a good starting point. We all relate to the world in our own unique way. However, spirituality starts becoming religious when spirituality takes on some of the characteristics of a particular religion. I bring my spirituality into the communal domain when it is tied into and influenced by community rituals arising from a shared faith narrative. With religious affiliation, at least theoretically, I'm both spiritual and religious. But I could be religious as a matter of convention rather than conviction. I could identify myself with a particular faith tradition without its spirituality.

Spirituality-without-religion can be a lonely space. The desire for solidarity and sharing is simply part of who we are. Some people dread the thought of eating alone in a restaurant. They desire not just the food but also the rich nourishment that comes from human contact. The loss of such contact during Covid-19 was one of the most severe trials for many.

This point is movingly and powerfully illustrated in *A Woman in Berlin*, written by an anonymous writer living through the terrifying experience of the Fall of Berlin in 1945 while living in the Russian zone. Life was not easy. While not affiliated to any religion, the author writes during one of her darkest hours that 'our spiritual need is great … our hearts have run dry, they're hungry for what the Catholic Church calls "manna" for the soul … I'd like to find a church next Sunday if I get the day off and they're having services … Those of us who don't belong to any church have to suffer alone in the darkness … I feel so hopelessly alone.' It's hard to find a better articulation of such spiritual loneliness in the absence of a supportive faith community, and how a faith community can be a conduit of solace to the religiously unaffiliated. It's as if they're carried on the shoulders of a faith community. She makes the case that while a private spirituality has its merits, the community dimension completes it. She also suggests that we all have a hunger for a spirituality. Our spirit needs to be nourished, and for many that involves being part of a community.

The famous advocacy journalist and radical bohemian social activist, Dorothy Day, in the aftermath of failed relationships and an abortion, feared that she could never have a child again. When her daughter Tamara was born a few years later to Dorothy and her common-law husband, Dorothy was not yet a Catholic. That would come later. The birth of her daughter was such a significant event for her that she said, 'No human creature could receive or contain so vast a flood of love and joy as I often felt after the birth of my child. With this came the need to worship, to adore.'[27] Here she expresses an intense spirituality of gratitude. 'The final object of this love and gratitude was God.'[28] She continues by saying that 'many wanted to worship God in their own way and did not need a church in which to praise him, nor a body of people with whom to associate themselves … My very experience as a radical [social activist], my whole make-up, led me to want to associate myself with others, the masses, in loving and praising God.'[29] She makes the point well about the support that being part of a faith tradition can give. She had her daughter Tamara baptised and became a Catholic herself, going on to become editor of *The Catholic Worker*, promoting Catholic social teaching and challenging conventional capitalism and its detrimental effects on the poorest and most vulnerable. Sticking to her principles and inspired by Gospel values she found herself behind bars on a number of occasions,

27. Dorothy Day, *The Long Loneliness*, New York, NY: HarperOne, 2017, p. 139.
28. Ibid.
29. Ibid.

experiencing at first hand what the poorest and most vulnerable had to suffer. Her cause for canonisation is under review. Those who have been emotionally and spiritually hurt by abortion could draw hope from her experience of forgiveness and making peace with her past.

Religions have their own brand of spirituality, their unique way of interpreting the meaning of human experience and expressing it through private and public prayer and familiar rituals. A religious community is bound together by binding beliefs. When the Jewish religion started, with its own way of understanding reality, it stood out in contrast to the prevailing religions of the time, especially in its novel expression of a strict monotheism, and the idea that God was involved in human history without undermining free will. Other religions had a multiplicity of gods. The Jewish people were often tempted to give up on their religion-with-spirituality because it didn't seem to be delivering what they were expecting. What's the point in believing in the Jewish God when going round in circles in a barren desert, searching for water in the scorching sunlight and getting nowhere? There was no place for people of other religions in the Jewish religion because there was a total conflict of spiritual understanding, with widely differing views on how to interpret the meaning of existence. In a nutshell, a religion is a community that shares a common faith narrative, expressed through rituals and embodied in a spirituality that gives meaning and direction to everyday life. For the Jews, their image of God, their sense of being chosen by God, the Torah, the Ten Commandments, were central to their identity. Their religious understanding dictated how life was to be ordered in order to facilitate the right relationship between God, between one another and the planet. Affiliation with a religion does not in any way diminish our personal way of relating to God and the world. The spirituality we profess is within a broader context than just ourselves.

Christianity grew out of its understanding of Jesus. It owes a huge debt of gratitude to Judaism for its wealth of spirituality, albeit nuanced by Christians in the light of Jesus' life, death and resurrection. During the centuries after the death and resurrection of Christ, there was intense reflection and study on the meaning of the Christ event and how it would play out in the spiritual lives of ordinary Christians, many of whom had been Jews. The content of the Christian religion worked itself out slowly and painfully, often against the background of contradictory understandings and disagreements which, over time, had to be settled once and for all. What exactly do Christians believe? It could reasonably be argued that the resurrection of Jesus was a bolt out of the blue and didn't quite fit with what his followers were expecting. This is suggested in John's Gospel, when the author remarks that when the friends of Jesus visited the tomb on Easter Sunday morning, their eyes were opened because until 'this moment they had failed to understand the teaching of scripture, that he must rise from the dead' (John 20). It was hard enough to explain a crucified Messiah, but the idea of resurrection was even more challenging. It's clear that finding a language to convey their experience was a huge linguistic challenge. How do you share your experience of the inexplicable? How do you explain the colour blue to a person unable to see? The Bible accounts highlight that their experience was not simply an inner subjective moment of profound insight without an objective reality. It is affirmed that the objective reality of the resurrection impacted on them. It was an intervention into their lives of someone outside of themselves. Therefore, it wasn't an invention coming from a subjective experience. However, what the experience was like is outside our comprehension. Belief in the resurrection rests on the trustworthiness of those who passed on their experience to us. Do I accept what this reported experience means, or do I reject it?

The growth of Christian understanding was painstakingly worked out in the New Testament as it attempted to interpret the life of Jesus, carefully reflecting on and alluding to reference points from the Old Testament, many of which have now faded from the memories of ordinary people. But the early Christians gradually began to understand the meaning of Jesus' life in the light of the Old Testament. They managed to get the point that the life of Jesus was the fulfilment of God's promise, which had been in preparation going back to the time of Abraham. Jesus didn't just appear out of the blue. It was the providential climax of preparation going back over hundreds of years. The Jewish people were chosen to have a unique role in that history. They were chosen by God to serve God's purpose. There was a delicate interplay between human freedom and God's design. Despite human waywardness, God's intention won out in the end without undermining human freedom.

As time moved on, some of the great ecumenical councils of the Christian community formulated the essentials of belief in credal formulas such as the Nicene Creed, which is accepted by all mainline Christian churches. A statement of belief had to be codified to articulate what Christians actually agreed on, what was essential if a person was to become a Christian. The Nicene Creed owes its origin to the Councils of Nicea (CE 325) and Constantinople (CE 381), now known respectively as Iznik and Istanbul in Turkey. The Emperor wanted to put a stop to all the religious bickering that was tearing communities apart about how to speak about God in the light of Jesus. However, understanding developed over time, even if it was quite complicated. The Christian community is a self-correcting one, where agreement on essentials is what binds it together. At no stage of these developments was 'blind faith' the arbiter of theological disputes. Today there is a misunderstanding among some that there is such a thing as 'blind faith'! Some of the best minds on the planet were involved in trying to guide the theological trajectory from its Jewish roots and the influence of Greek philosophy to Christianity, while maintaining the strict monotheism of the Jewish and Christian traditions. The richness of Jewish theology played an essential role in interpreting the meaning of the Christ event, as did Greek philosophy, leading eventually to the affirmation of the Christian God as Trinity, a challenging and difficult balancing act. Christians struggle with language when trying to talk about God because God is beyond human understanding. God is simply ineffable, beyond understanding. We can only work with limited knowledge, in the knowledge that anything we say about God is limited anyway and that there is as much unsaid as said. It's impossible to comprehend the incomprehensible. We make the most of the shafts of light to glimpse the mystery of God. Therefore, our 'Concepts, words must not become screens; they must be regarded as windows',[30] allowing a glimpse of the ultimate mystery. It's always wise to be cautious when church leaders and others claim to know with certainty what God thinks!

The point, therefore, is that religions are communities that share a common belief that inspires spirituality. Religious participation provides the community dimension for people who share a common story

30. Abraham Joshua Heschel, op. cit., Amazon Kindle edition, p. 116.

that binds them together. Religious rituals provide the spiritual space to become immersed in rereading and paying attention to the common heritage. Spirituality focuses on the 'I', whereas religion focuses on the 'we'. As in marriage, it's a question of finding the right balance between the two. Spirituality and religion enrich one another. Traditional faith stories play an invaluable role in people's lives and support them through the inevitable struggles that come their way.

When it comes to spirituality and religion, we don't need to reinvent the wheel. There is a rich tradition of religious faith that has survived over thousands of years against the odds. For those trying to forge a spirituality, the many traditions have much to teach us. We don't have to start from scratch. The wisdom of the ages is there for us to embrace. We walk in the footsteps of great religious giants who stayed the course despite persecutions and temptations to infidelity and despair.

As in other religious traditions, there are at least three elements to Christian religion, sometimes popularised as head, heart and hands. The 'head' is the content of belief expressed in creeds, the Bible, teachings and traditions. These involve the various intellectual propositions to which a person gives assent. At a christening ceremony, parents and godparents are asked to affirm the essentials of Christian faith immediately before the baptismal candidate has the blessed water poured over their head, in the name of the Father, and of the Son and of the Holy Spirit, the traditional Trinitarian formula going way back to the first days of Christianity. However, it goes without saying, as already indicated, that we can never fully comprehend God. Consequently, we will have unanswered and unanswerable questions. Faith and doubt will coexist. God cannot be defined by human categories. God has God's own meaning. For everything we say about God, there is more to explore. God cannot be boxed in. Defining God includes accepting the fact that we cannot define. No human mind can ever know everything there is to be known! Even if we did know everything, there is a further question. Why is there anything to be known anyway? A doubting, questioning faith is a sign of a healthy and humble faith. In his great poem 'In Memoriam', Alfred Lord Tennyson wrote that 'There lives more faith in honest doubt, / Believe me, than in half the creeds.' A doubting faith, far from being a problem, is a creative gift, and a sign of strength, indicating that a person can embrace ambiguity. It stimulates the intellect and challenges us to do some serious enquiry about the area of doubt that bothers us. We don't know as much as we think we do, which reminds us that we are part of something greater than ourselves. The 'head' is the intellectual dimension of religion, facilitating religious and biblical literacy. Some believers will have an avid interest in this, which is to be admired, as religious literacy is on the wane. On the other hand, many will be happy on their faith journey with a minimum level of theological enquiry because what they already know serves them well. They may pray regularly; there is an old Latin tag, *'Lex orandi, lex credendi'*, which means that the prayers of the community embed the beliefs of the community which, in turn, influence lifestyle.

A rigid, fundamental and unquestioning faith, which is unable to live with unanswered questions and ambiguities, insults our rationality and the implicit drive within to work things out. There's always more to know and understand where the content of faith is concerned. It's not a closed 'deposit of faith', like a suitcase full of answers to puzzles that we carry around with us. Unfortunately, this image has defined faith in the past. Theologians who rocked the boat found themselves in deep water. Theological novelty was outlawed. Better to fossilise Christianity was the approach. However, such an approach is destructive to the Gospel message. Faith invites continuing conversation with an evolving world. We were given our mental faculties for a good reason. It stimulates enquiry. Each new generation brings new questions to faith. We reread our common story through a contemporary lens to understand how it applies in our concrete situation. Thankfully, that's always going to generate a creative tension. St Paul may have wanted women to wear a head covering during religious services in his first-century culture, but we've come a long way since then! St Paul may have tolerated slavery, but any right-thinking person today would abhor it. The history and development of Christian doctrines confirm that teaching and understanding develop. The great councils of Christianity were tasked with formulating a response to contemporary questions. The encounter between culture and Christianity refined, developed and clarified what the community believed. The great theologian Anselm of Canterbury coined the phrase, *'Fides quaerens intellectum'*, meaning faith seeks understanding. We do that by employing our intellect. This is an essential and appropriate activity. Contrary to misleading perceptions such as 'blind faith', the content of faith came about through careful and sometimes bitter intellectual struggles.

The experience of the 'heart' comes closer to what is more popularly meant by spirituality. The Nicene Creed, recited on Sundays, starts with, 'I believe in God.' I can believe in God in the sense of a credal formula. I believe that certain statements about God are true. It is primarily information about God, the 'head' part of faith. However, 'I believe in God' can also move beyond an affirmation of statements to a relationship of trust in the person believed in, God, because that person has been shown to be trustworthy. It's an affirmation of trust in God's friendship and fidelity, with its implications for a person's lifestyle. 'I believe in God' suggests commitment of the whole person. There is a difference between knowing about God and knowing God by heart. Significant personal relationships are based on trust and can be betrayed, but God's fidelity is guaranteed. Such is the conviction of biblical truth based on compelling evidence. I can give up on God, but God never gives up on me. This is at the heart of the Eucharist, when the words used by Jesus ratifying the new covenant (agreement) are spoken aloud.

Commercial relationships are also based on trust. When I step on board an aircraft, I make an act of trust in the pilot. It is reasonable to presume she has the required skills and certification to fly. I don't try to barge into the cockpit asking to see her pilot's licence. If I do, I will end up in a hospital or in court, if I'm not shot at by security guards. When I believe in God, I place my trust in a trustworthy person and express that trust through prayerful activity, such as gratitude and praise, praying for others and myself, and entrusting the sorrows of the world into the care of God. This trust can be hard, especially when everything around me is becoming undone and will challenge a lifestyle of trust in God.

There's an inspiring passage from the Book of Habakkuk where the author describes the attitude of a person whose world has come

44

apart – they have lost their livelihood and income, everything! The bottom has fallen out of their world, as happens to countless numbers of people every day, especially in war zones and many other areas of life. Yet the author, faced with such a huge calamity, can still say, 'Yet I will rejoice in the Lord / and exult in God my saviour / The Lord my God is my strength' (Habakkuk 3:18–19). That is just one of extraordinary acts of trust in God found throughout the Bible. That's the kind of faith involved in 'I believe in God.' At such times many of us may not be able to make such an act of trust as it seems to defy the odds. We simply allow ourselves to be carried along by the prayerful trust of our faith community, as if we're stowaways on their prayers. Experience also confirms that those with a deep, trusting faith are supported by their conviction that God can be relied on especially during difficult times, because the Bible reassures us that God is on the side of the broken-hearted.

The 'heart' also involves at least some personal prayer on a regular basis. It includes learning how to meditate on biblical texts. Ignatius of Loyola teaches us different methods of prayer in his Spiritual Exercises. He suggests taking a Jesus narrative from the Gospels and entering the scene as if we were participants in the event. The power of imagination can transform our friendship with God and deepen our understanding. We can also take a psalm and stop when something strikes us and mull over it, paying attention to what's going on in the heart while we listen to God and respond in our own words. There are as many ways of praying as there are people, and finding our prayer style as a bridge to God is a gift. Some like to walk on the seashore or a rugged mountain and taste the beauty of creation while reciting a psalm as background music to help articulate wonder at the greatness and mystery of the universe. Many are put off by prayer in the false belief that they must wear their Sunday best before God. We come to God as we are, warts and all, in the same way that we go to a doctor for healing remedies. It's not a case of cleaning the house before the cleaners come. It's a friendship where airs and graces are off limits because we might be able to fool ourselves, but we can't fool God. It's helpful to remember that God loves us not for our good deeds, but for who we are, a member of God's family, even if we're not conscious of that reality. It's like the parent who loves their child even before they have achieved anything. What matters is that this child is their son or daughter, their own flesh and blood, and blood is always thicker than water. Such is our relationship with God. One of the gifts of parenthood is that children teach us what it's like to be vulnerable, dependent and full of wonder. God wants us to incorporate these traits into our friendship with him.

A cloistered nun was asked why she prayed. 'Because I breathe,' she replied.[31] People want to pray because 'they want to experience God's extraordinary presence in their ordinary lives'.[32] However, prayer demands 'a slow and deliberate effort, a dedicated time for reflection, and an authentic response from our soul'.[33] The effect of prayer is to see with the heart and respond appropriately. It brings peace to the spirit and facilitates the welling up in the heart of compassion, empathy, gratitude and hope. We also bring others before God as our way of supporting them through good times and bad.

At times of crisis and suffering, such as a funeral, when people gather, they pray the Rosary. For many the predictable rote recitation of the prayers is soothing background music as they mourn their loved one. The rhythmic gentle murmuring of the prayers is comforting and at least reassures us that we are doing something for the deceased. However, perhaps it's time to consider adding to the repertoire of the praying community by the rote learning of other prayers, such as the prayer of Zechariah, John the Baptist's father. This prayer reminds us how much a tender-hearted God has done for humanity. The promise made to Abraham was fulfilled and reinforces how trustworthy God is. Some psalms could also be learned by heart. Rote learning of scripture facilitates the movement of what's in the head to the heart, which is a different way of experiencing scripture. If we learn scripture by heart it stays with us for ever and can be a comfort in a time of need.

'Hands' is the metaphor for the performative element of a particular religion, which includes a commitment to reaching out to others, caring for family and friends, service projects, contributing to the welfare of the wider community and all those other acts of generosity and kindness that

31. John Delli Carpini, *Poetry as Prayer – Emily Dickinson*, Boston, MA: Pauline Books and Media, 2002, p. 7.
32. Ibid.
33. Ibid.

support the realisation of a healthy and just community. This is succinctly expressed in a Christian context by that feisty Spanish nun, St Teresa of Ávila, when she writes, 'Yours are the hands, yours are the feet, yours are the eyes, you are his body. Christ has no body now on earth but yours.' The community of the baptised constitutes the body of Christ, continuing where Christ left off in the knowledge that it's goodness that will have the last word. It's easy to fall into despair when we listen to the news headlines. It seems as if things are going from worse to worse. The temptation to hopelessness comes from a bad space. It forgets that the resurrection guarantees the final victory of good over evil. Therefore, the good that we do is never lost. There will still be plenty of battles on the way, but victory is assured. The challenge is to hang in there, playing our limited role as best we can, in the knowledge that the good that we do will flourish and will constitute part of that great tapestry of life. However, the good that we do doesn't always yield an instant harvest. As farmers and gardeners know only too well it often takes time for the good seeds we have sown to flourish, but, thankfully, 'all the good fruits of our nature and enterprise, we will find them again, but freed from stain, burnished and transfigured'.[34] This is a profound and encouraging interpretation of life's meaning. Playwright Dorothy Sayers expresses a similar sentiment when one of her characters says, 'There is no waste with God; He cancels nothing / But redeems all.'[35] Aesop had a similar insight nearly 600 years before Christ in his fable 'The Lion and the Mouse', where he reinforced the idea that no act of kindness, no matter how small, is ever wasted. Therefore, anything good we do to create a hope-filled world for our young people is never done in vain, even if it appears so at the time. It's reassuring to know that the good that we do will outlast us.

Ideally these three aspects of religion coalesce in a person, and for many religious people they do so, with perhaps one or other of the three features getting more attention than others. Where Christianity is concerned, many people are excellent at the 'hands' dimension, serving the needs of the those who have lost their way, caring for their

34. Walter Abbott, *The Documents of Vatican II*, New York, NY: The America Press, 1966, p. 237.
35. In Gerald O'Collins, *Interpreting Jesus*, London: Mowbray, 1992, p. 127.

families and others in a generous way, but don't explicitly make the connection between such self-giving and the other two parts. However, a person doesn't have to be a top-class theologian to live a deep faith. A minimal grasp of the essentials of faith may be adequate to animate an individual's faith. Others may prefer to delve deeper to have a better understanding of what it's all about. It depends to some extent on temperament.

The 'head,' is the shared vision coming from a particular way of talking about God. The 'heart' includes personal and common prayer in response to God's desire to befriend each of us. The 'hands' express a lifestyle inspired by our personal and communal relationship with God. Christianity, Judaism and Islam have at least these three foundations. Religion, therefore, helps to structure and inform our spirituality while leaving a lot of flexibility as each person relates to God in their own unique way within a religious context. We have our own personal style of being in friendship with God. Our personal experience of God is unique to us. Through regular, shared worship experiences, we support one another and highlight the communal aspect of spirituality, just as we reinforce the communal aspect of so many other areas of life. It's not surprising, therefore, that so many want to make their pilgrim way to the top of Croagh Patrick on the last Sunday of July with others who share the same goal, even though their reasons may be quite personal. The presence of others on the pilgrim trail strengthens our commitment and is a source of support when the mountain, like life itself, gets tough. The Croagh Patrick pilgrimage in some ways serves as a metaphor for the link between spirituality and religion. It has a way of binding people together through the story of its long history and rituals, while at the same time providing a context for the expression of spirituality. Pilgrims walk in the footsteps of countless pilgrims, becoming part of something bigger than themselves. Like religion itself, there is the 'I' and the 'we.' The banter, the fun and the prayers at the summit keep us on our toes. A similar dynamic is at work on the Camino de Santiago.

Many Catholic Christians have given up on the faith they were brought up in, especially in the Western world. There is a variety of reasons for this, some of which we saw in the introduction. There is also the failure of leadership in dealing appropriately with abuse scandals, which have generated intense anger and disillusionment. It could also be argued that it would be more honest 'to blame religion for its own defeats ... when faith becomes an heirloom rather than a living fountain; when religion speaks only in the name of authority rather than with the voice of compassion – its message becomes meaningless'.[36] Yet there is also a much deeper issue. If religion is an answer to our ultimate questions about life and its meaning, it could also be argued that 'the moment we become oblivious to ultimate questions, religion becomes irrelevant, and its crisis sets in'.[37] The rejection of religion is, therefore, a multi-layered complex issue.

Against this background, identification with the Catholic Christian community is simply not an option for many. Catholic Christianity is often increasingly regarded by many as simply irrelevant to contemporary struggles. It seems to have nothing meaningful to say. It's perceived by many as being unable sensitively and creatively to respond to sexual concerns about which we now have a more developed and nuanced understanding that biblical authors didn't have. The people in the pews are voting with their feet and exiting.

Doing church, the way we always did, doesn't work anymore. The Church in Ireland and other places is operating in a new socio-cultural milieu where people are well-educated, constantly busy, think for themselves and, increasingly, don't identify as religious. Gone are the days of a patriarchal, clerical, authoritarian Catholic Church, when the people in the pews had to pray, pay and obey. The consequence of this is that challenging decisions must be made about how we do church. This is the most pressing challenge facing the international Church. Pastors, with the 'smell of the sheep', ministering in the 'field hospital' church need to accompany the sheep, listening attentively and sharing the concerns and questions of the flock. There is no place for an arrogant pastor. The pastor is also a pilgrim on the way, sharing the human condition, the strengths and weaknesses of his own humanity, a sinner like everyone else, loved by God, and who doesn't have all the answers. With a decrease in the number of priests, promoting the current clerical model by importing ordained ministers does no one any service. It postpones the necessity of

36. Abraham Joshua Heschel, op. cit., Amazon Kindle edition, p. 3.
37. Ibid.

lay leadership and collaboration and procrastinates about the theology and practice of ministerial priesthood. As our understanding of Church deepens, it's a short-sighted solution to a long-term problem.

The thorny question of who a candidate for priestly ordination can be needs to be honestly and critically addressed, especially if there is to be a consistency between what Church leaders say and do. They speak about the paramount importance of the Eucharist without encouraging novel and courageous ways to have Eucharistic presiders, the result of which is to deprive the baptised of Eucharistic food on the often harsh and challenging journey of life. If the Eucharist is as important as Jesus and the Church say it is, then there is an urgent priority to authorise Eucharistic presiders outside the current clerical model, especially in remote areas. Imaginative creativity is required here, especially given the fact that once people are deprived of Eucharist, their Christian affiliation becomes less robust or anaemic. There needs to be a different model of priesthood in collaboration with the lay baptised. And the concept of territorial parishes, focused on a physical building, in many cases may need to yield to other forms of ecclesial communities.

Some in the highest echelons of the Church challenge the traditional clerical model with its one-size-fits-all understanding of who's eligible for ministerial priesthood, which is a welcome and overdue change. Presuming that the sacrament of ordination confers administrative, financial, spiritual, people and management skills on a person is a mistake. Clerics and laity need to work together, sharing responsibility, each according to their gifts. This creates challenges, such as the possibility of ordaining married men and unmarried and married women in the context of a developed and novel model of sacramental priesthood. It's anomalous how a woman can baptise in the case of an emergency in the name of Christ, but can't preside at the Eucharist in the name of Christ. A somewhat dubious theology of the presider being the same gender as Christ has stymied the debate. However, where there's a will, there's a way. It's too easy to give in to despair about the future, which presents novel opportunities, but time is running out before Christianity implodes, becoming something students will read about in historical textbooks. Like climate change, it's happening before our very eyes, as we fiddle while Rome and the planet burn.

The boat has moved out of the harbour, and under the legacy of Pope Francis's guidance is moving in a new direction. If synodality gains traction we will have a more challenging, decentralised and exciting model of church. Many will be left behind because they will have a fossilised view of church and will look backwards to an imagined golden age of elaborate liturgies and other trappings that have outlived their purpose. It's no coincidence that widescale abuse occurred during that so-called golden age, with its obsessive focus on sexual morality and ritual purity such as the 'churching' of women after birth. The 'churching' of women after the last Mass on a Sunday is a bizarre memory from my boyhood that still stands out. All the women of the parish who had given birth were expected to turn up for this ritual. What was this saying to women? The miracle and joy of birth, along with their generosity in welcoming new life, were tainted by the idea of ritual impurity! On the one hand, the Church was telling married couples to have babies and, on the other, that childbirth was a ritually impure process!

It's not surprising that Pope Francis restricted the Latin Mass, which can be aesthetic but theologically outmoded, hijacked in some circles to foster disharmony and protest, expropriating the Eucharist for ecclesial politics. Burying the head in the sand like an ostrich won't serve the Church. Even the first Christians had to engage with the culture to find the best means of communicating the novel Christian message. The challenge initially was how to preach to those influenced by Greek philosophy and Jews wishing to be Christians. If they hadn't done so in a creative and responsible way, Christianity would have died the death at the outset.

Sadly, only a minority study theology to degree level. Theology is a challenging discipline, like other college subjects, demanding high academic standards and a personal capacity for serious intellectual commitment. Theology focuses on how different religions understand and talk about God. The term 'theology' owes its origin to the French philosopher Peter Abelard. Any serious student of theology will quickly debunk the myth of 'blind faith'. They will see that such a position insults rationality and undermines professional academic competence. It comes as a surprise to many that some of the most prestigious universities in the world support a theology faculty, such as the Harvard Divinity School. There is a generally accepted point of view in our culture that one uninformed opinion is as good as another where religious debate is concerned. Media talk shows often illustrate this, with the sharing of opinions where one opinion is regarded as valid as any other, no matter how uninformed. And, whether you're informed or not, you must accept it! That's not how we operate in other complex areas of life. A pilot flying a plane does so strictly by the book. If a flight is determined only by a pilot's opinion and sensory perception the airways would soon be lethal. There is plenty of documentation to highlight the fact that some aircraft crashed because the pilots ignored their instruments in favour of their mistaken opinions about sensory perception, not realising how disoriented they were. This was particularly true in the case of the US mail planes in the early days of flight. Instruments were sometimes ignored in favour of disoriented perception. Agreed operating protocols must now be followed. Covid-19 protests are sometimes informed by misguided information about vaccines and conspiracy theories that have no foundation in fact. This dynamic is well documented in the TV series *Borat's American Lockdown*, which highlights what happens in the absence of critical reflection.

To illustrate the foolishness of basing opinions on fantasy and to tease my students, I would sometimes say that in my opinion, a man was left behind on the moon after the first moon landing in 1969. Someone closed the hatch of the spacecraft too quickly as it was preparing to return to earth. Only half-way back to earth did any one notice what had happened. That man could be seen on the moon every night waving a banner that said, 'Save Me. They left me behind!' That's my opinion, and you must respect it! The use of reason highlights the foolishness of such a position. Yet we live in a world of 'alternative facts', as popularised by the Trump White House. What else can we expect? Without academic rigour, including the study of philosophy and especially epistemology (how do I know that I know?), objectivity and truth will continue to be replaced by relativism and other 'isms' that undermine immanent intelligibility, a linguistic jawbreaker meaning that things-in-themselves have their own meaning apart from what I think. None of us likes to be misunderstood and judged by other people. It's a common phenomenon. Those with a superficial knowledge of us can quickly label us. They ignore the depth of our reality with their superficial assessment and miss the meaning of who we really are. We all have our own immanent intelligibility, regardless of what others think they know about us, especially when they only know the half of it – but they don't realise that.

This concept is particularly important when discussing God. If I come to the debate having already made up my mind about God, or unaware of my emotional and intellectual blind spots, then my conclusions may be flawed. I impose my perceptions on God and ignore God's immanent intelligibility, not letting him get a word in edgewise. Rejection of God is often inspired by emotions such as anger rather than intellectual reasons. If God is supposed to be good, why did such-and-such a thing happen that has ruined our lives? Why do I have this debilitating cancer? Why do bad things happen to good people? On the God question we often bring our limited human ideas to impose on God, even though there is so much that we will never be able to understand. As previously pointed out, those who don't believe in a god often reject a god that believers also reject. We ask how a loving God could 'send' someone to hell. It's a complex question with an equally complex way of answering that goes beyond the soundbite. Yet the bottom line is simple enough. God doesn't sit on the judgment seat sending people to hell every other minute. It's more complicated than that. In brief, it highlights issues about human responsibility and the consequences of my actions. It's as much a philosophical question as a god question. The Catholic Church doesn't say that anyone is in hell. It acknowledges the fact that a person is free to cut themselves off from being loved and loving others if they so wish. Hell is a technical term for the deliberate choice to inhabit a loveless space. God respects our decisions because he does not force himself on us.

Surprisingly, what Christians and those who don't believe in God find even more difficult to believe is the capacity of God to forgive. It's all right for God to forgive the people I think should be forgiven. However, let's be realistic and not stretch the boundaries. The German Rudolf Hoess was baptised a Catholic. He lived in a claustrophobic, smothering Catholic household where his pious and strict father wanted him to be a priest. However, over time young Rudolf became estranged from the Catholic Church and eventually became the commandant of the

Auschwitz-Birkenau extermination camp, where at least three million people died on his watch. He was uncritically swept off his feet and caught up in the Nazi nightmare masquerading as a dream. At the end of the war, he was sentenced to death. In the days prior to his execution, he could hear the bells calling the nearby Carmelite sisters to prayer. He began to acknowledge how he had seriously sinned against God and humanity and wanted God's forgiveness in the sacrament of reconciliation. He was given permission to meet Fr Wladyslaw Lohn SJ, who heard his confession. On 16 April 1947, he was permitted to receive Viaticum, his final communion before death. He explained in a letter to his family how difficult he found the struggle to reconnect with his childhood faith. His conviction that he had been forgiven was also evident, even though at the same time he acknowledged that humanity might not be able to forgive him, which was a wise perception. We think of all those families impacted by his inhumanity and the intensity of the devastation, desolation and anger they experienced. When I used to relate this story, it would be met with all kinds of objections on the 'eye for an eye, tooth for a tooth' retaliatory philosophy, which is totally understandable. Our natural tendency is to put limits on whom we forgive. Revenge is ingrained in Christians as much as anyone else. All we need to do is scratch the surface. Forgiving those who have seriously wronged us is close to impossible in many situations. The hurt of the damage done to us is too much. We think of all those killed, maimed and having to flee their homes in Ukraine and the personal and collective devastation that has ensued. It's not difficult to empathise with bitterness and anger. Many of us have significant examples from our own lives of justifiable anger and an unwillingness to forgive. Yet how we handle those experiences is what counts.

How could God forgive Rudolf Hoess? Surely that's enough to put anyone off Christianity? Many would understandably argue that he should be in hell. During a talk at a retreat, the Jesuit retreat director was heard to say that the biggest block to being a Christian was the teaching on forgiveness. When people hear the Rudolf Hoess story, they are incredulous. Perhaps the Jesuit retreat director was right. Isn't there something in the Lord's prayer about forgiveness? It's something we need to pray for. On the cross Jesus forgave his enemies, an action many of us may have difficulties with. On our own cross where we have been unjustly crucified, we can find it difficult. Jesus forgave because that's the only thing that made sense to him. That's what God does. God cannot do otherwise. If a repentant person asks for forgiveness, God gives it. God's forgiveness threshold is a high bar for humans. Holding on to resentment breeds resentment and anger. Failure to forgive means we become victims of an angry resentment that gnaws away at us, giving the person who perpetuated the original injustice a twofold stranglehold over us. We give power to the aggressor. Because forgiveness can be so hard and beyond our grasp, God knows we need to pray for it. If it's impossible for us to forgive, we can pray for the desire to do so as a starting point. We need to be patient with ourselves and forgive ourselves for our inability to forgive, but in the expectation that, with God's grace, the day will come when we can finally let go of the immense burden, handing grief, resentment and anger over to the crucified Jesus. History has demonstrated the devastation of tit-for-tat reprisals. The Christian message where forgiveness is concerned is tough. Is there a better way? Giving negative release to pent-up anger at perceived or real offences creates more problems than it solves. Jesus has highlighted the priority of short-circuiting the vicious cycle of recrimination. Yet, in the middle of a crisis, we don't act rationally. That's why Ignatius of Loyola stresses the importance of making decisions only when in a good space where we can reflect on our thoughts and feelings. Perhaps if we lived in a less angry world, we would inhabit a more peaceful world.

When we go to a medical consultant, we expect them to be proficient in their speciality. Yet, in the religious sphere, it's anything goes, without hard evidence or argument. There is a view that the intellectual content of Christianity is simply a set of propositions that were somehow composed willy-nilly, somewhat along the lines of a young child doodling on a piece of paper. Nothing could be further from the truth. The Christian creed and biblical studies satisfy all the criteria for the most rigorous and painstaking scholarship. This is how it should be, because many of us have staked our lives on the veracity of the Christian message, rigorously thought through by our ancestors, and passed from one generation to another, albeit with each generation engaging critically with the essential content of faith and even modifying the non-essentials where appropriate and casting a new light on how the essentials might be understood. St Paul reminds us that if the resurrection didn't happen, we are the sorriest of people because, if 'there is no resurrection of the dead, Christ himself cannot have been raised, and if Christ has not been raised then our preaching is useless and your believing it is useless; indeed, we are shown up as witnesses who have committed perjury before God because we swore in evidence before God that he had raised Christ to life' (1 Corinthians 15:13–16). This is a powerful statement asserting the resurrection, the foundational event for Christianity. Without the fact of the resurrection, there can be no Christianity. Everything stems from that. A Christian makes an act of trust in those who have reported their experience of resurrection because the resurrection is not a historical fact, it is a fact of personal experience given to some and shared with others.

It's particularly disturbing to meet educated Catholics, leaders in their chosen profession, who have severed their relationship with the Church community because their personal faith has not moved beyond what they learned in primary school. It was an age-related faith that simply failed to flourish. Even St Paul in his letter to the Christians of Corinth wrote, 'you are not to be childish in your outlook ... but mentally you must be adult' (1 Corinthians 14:20). They read the story of Adam and Eve and highlight what they regard as its nonsense, given what we know about evolution, but fail to recognise the purpose of biblical narrative. Another chapter will address this issue. That is not to say that Church scholarship has sometimes been mistaken, which isn't surprising – the Christian community as much as any other group is influenced by the culture of the day and inherits societal blind spots. The Christian support for slavery, or Christian colonialists rejecting indigenous culture come to mind. Therefore, the Christian community needs always to be in a reflective self-correcting mode, supported by theologians and the lived experience of the ordinary person in the pew, whose wisdom is invaluable if it's allowed to be heard! Perhaps synodality will correct this imbalance. Theologian Daniel Horan states that 'church teaching develops and, in fact, changes. It doesn't happen often, but teaching has and ought to change when we realise that the remote possibility of error in non-fallible teaching is discovered. The Church's view on slavery and religious liberty are just two of many examples where this has been the case. And it is likely that the current institutional views on the treatment of LGBTQ individuals not only should but will also change.'[38]

Niall Williams, in his novel *This is Happiness*, makes a profound observation on those whose faith is no longer fit for purpose. He writes, 'When you've been raised inside a religion, it's not a small thing to step outside it. Even if you no longer believe in it, you can feel its absence. There's a spirit-wound to a Sunday. You can patch it, but it's there, whether natural or invented, not for me to say.'[39] Putting religious affiliation aside can be like binning an old pair of shoes that don't quite fit. This raises questions about the quality of the rejected faith in the first place. Handing on the faith at baptism, First Communion and Confirmation is more than just a 'nice' cultural custom. It involves an invitation to ownership.

How many ever experience the rejection of their childhood faith as a 'spirit-wound'? It's a profound metaphor. It highlights that we are spiritual beings and that it's in our DNA to thirst for God. We manage to ignore the 'spirit-wound' if it's not bothering us, which is often the case as the urgent short-term and long-term preferences take over our lives. If the wound is bandaged and not drawing attention to itself, we're fine, but occasionally, life events will sting the wound and we will, at least vaguely, feel its tingling sensation provoking questions about life's meaning.

Perhaps the wound tingles a little bit at Christmas, explaining why so many people like to participate in religious services. We enjoy the support of community, meet friends and neighbours within the context of religious affiliation. Perhaps more is going on. Maybe we unconsciously yearn for lost innocence and a deeper faith inspired by the atmosphere of Christmas Mass and carols. We experience an intuition of original innocence and blessing that is hard to articulate. The wound we usually ignore begins to smart a little. The more spiritual side of Christmas has the capacity to reignite that spark of innocent childhood faith and wonder, expressed by the poet Dylan Thomas in his poem 'Fern Hill': 'Now as I was young and easy under the apple bows / About the lilting house and happy as the grass was green.'

38. *National Catholic Reporter*, 9 February 2022.
39. Niall Williams, *This is Happiness*, London: Bloomsbury Publishing, 2019, p. 107.

The power of the Christmas story and the image of the crib speak volumes and can trigger a spiritual yearning. Christmas has a way of touching our vulnerable humanity in unexpected ways, evoking a nostalgia for an innocence we can't quite get our head around. Is this God's way of drawing attention to our 'spirit-wound'? God's way of communicating with us is through our feelings, as St Ignatius of Loyola teaches. Our task is to pay attention. Perhaps that obscured spiritual sense, against the background of the various expectations of Christmas, feeds into the anxiety and tension that are also commonplace at Christmas. Someone beyond ourselves is tugging at the heartstrings, trying to get us to listen in the depths of the heart where God speaks to us quietly, undramatically and gently, drawing attention to that 'spirit-wound' tingling away beneath our consciousness. All we must do is pay attention to what we're hearing and where it's leading us to. The gift of Christmas is the removal of the bandage to let the 'spirit-wound' heal. Denis O'Driscoll highlights this uninvited yearning in his poem 'Missing God'. He writes: 'Yet, though we rebelled against Him / like adolescents, uplifted to see / an oppressive father banished – /a bearded hermit – to the desert, / we confess to missing Him at times.' He then continues, beginning most of the remaining stanzas with the phrase 'Miss him when ... ', giving examples of moments when a triggering of a deep yearning for a missed God can occur. 'Miss him when a choked voice at / the crematorium recites the poem / about fearing no more the heat of the sun.'[40]

Maybe the spirituality and belief system that are jettisoned aren't so irrelevant after all. Just maybe, Christmas and other experiences become the conduit for seeing things from a slightly different perspective and for developing an adult understanding of what has been thrown overboard in the belief that it was all mumbo jumbo anyway. Patrick Kavanagh puts it well when he writes about what will occur after the Advent season, 'When the dry black bread and the sugarless tea / Of penance will charm back the luxury / Of a child's soul ... '[41] The innocence of the child loses its lustre

40. Denis O'Driscoll, *Exemplary Damages*, London: Anvil Press Poetry, 2002, p. 29.
41. Peter Kavanagh (ed.), *Patrick Kavanagh: The Complete Poems*, Newbridge, The Goldsmith Press, 1988, p. 124.

as the child individuates. The innocence we're born with quickly becomes tainted and what we long for in life becomes obscured by the rat race.

It was the French Jesuit philosopher, theologian and palaeontologist, Pierre Teilhard de Chardin, who came up with the suggestion that we are spiritual beings having a human experience. It's not surprising that we're primed to be spiritual seekers. Like the needle on a compass, we're pointed in the right direction to reconnect with who we really are. Spirituality and religion can help us along the path. Travelling alone on challenging rugged tracks involves more risks than travelling with others. Spirituality is like travelling alone, whereas religion is like travelling together, sharing the same map and compass. There's safety in numbers and support in the event of getting lost in the dark where hungry bears may be lurking in the woods. We are persons-in-relationship, and we also are connected to the huge legacy of human wisdom accumulated throughout the ages, reinforcing that the search for truth is communal. No individual can be the sole arbiter of truth because such a dynamic is too self-referent. In academic disciplines, researchers publish their material to be reviewed by their peers, engaging with the wider intellectual community to test and validate their research.

Ultimately, the question of spirituality and religion has got to do with the very deepest longings of the heart. When all the superficial layers of life are stripped away, status, prestige, image, possessions, what others think of me, the masks I wear, the roles I play, the most significant questions, as I mentioned in another book, are:

- Where have I come from?
- Who am I?
- Where am I going?
- How do I get there?
- What do I really want along the way?[42]

These five questions implicitly include the God-question, or the transcendent, which is a technical term for all that's beyond our sensory experience. Human beings are each unique in their own way, but they also share so much in common. There is a lot of similarity in the way

42. Jim Maher, op. cit., p. 28.

the preceding questions will be answered. The answers to those questions inform a person's personal spirituality against the background of questions about ultimate reality, such as the person we call God, and the meaning of existence. Those with a similar spirituality often find a home in a specific religion that supports their spiritual quest. While being spiritual is a wonderful human experience, the quality of spirituality can be enriched by a particular religious affiliation where we're bound together by a shared story leading to mutual support, community, social and climate justice, intellectual enquiry and prayerful expression.

Religion	Travelling with others
Religion-with-spirituality	Immersed in common story
Head	Content of belief – religious literacy
Heart	God-connection – prayer rituals
Hands	Justice – creating a hope-filled future for young people in our common home

CHAPTER 3

Fanciful Thinking

There are many narratives in the Bible that defy credibility and raise some awkward questions. Does that mean the Bible is nonsense and that my Bible-based faith must therefore be rejected? How about all those people who take every event in the Bible literally, as if things happened the way they are described? How could the Red Sea suddenly part, facilitating safe passage for Jewish slaves on the run from Egypt? Come on! We're no longer in the Stone Age!

A way forward is simply to understand how to read and interpret the scriptures through the study of literary forms, figurative language, socio-cultural context, historical data, target audience and the purpose of a text. Thankfully, the Leaving Certificate syllabus encourages students to distinguish between different literary genres and different language modes. Students are taught about the significance of the target audience and how to assess the purpose of a text, all tools that are necessary for biblical study. Biblical literary criticism is not unlike literary criticism in many respects.

When we read a fable, we're not surprised that animals speak. That's the convention. Everybody knows that! When we're watching Disney's *Lion King*, we accept the narrative convention that animals can speak and act like humans. Therefore, to avoid a literal, fundamentalist understanding of the Bible, we need to be aware that it is a complex book which incorporates many different literary genres and historical and traditional reference points to articulate the Jewish and Christian faith. As a work of literature, it is a masterpiece. The Bible is not a history book in the accepted sense. Old Testament biblical references are found throughout the New Testament, which helped the early Jewish Christians to interpret the Jesus-event in the light of the Old Testament. The references were well-known to Christians who started out their lives as Jews. They are lost on contemporary Christians unless we have a comprehensive understanding of the Bible, which is often not the case. It's a bit like the references we have in Irish culture. 'That would be an ecumenical matter!' Most Irish people of a certain age recognise Fr Jack's phrase from the *Father Ted* series. Or the phrase 'brown envelope', which epitomises an era of sleaze and corruption in Irish politics when bribery was the order of the day and ill-gotten gains were handed over in brown envelopes. Or Teresa Mannion's plea to her television viewers during a raging storm not to make unnecessary journeys, which has entered folklore, or the annual *Late Late Toy Show*, or Michael O'Leary, synonymous with Ryanair. Every culture has its well-known reference points many of which fade over time and are replaced by others. For twenty-first century people, most of the references Old Testament Jews knew like the back of their hand are a mystery. That makes bible-reading challenging and sometimes demands hard work.

When the account of creation is recounted in the book of Genesis, the first book of the Bible, we know that it's not a historical account and that the narrative is modelled on an ancient literary form. The literary genre of the myth, with its recognisable style, is employed to convey the Jewish understanding of their God and the origin of the cosmos. Unfortunately, the term myth in common contemporary usage and understanding can suggest something that is untrue. In ancient times myths were used in different religions to convey a faith community's understanding of how the world began. A myth was an established form of conveying complex ideas following recognisable literary patterns.

Just like the other tribes, the Jews would reflect on their faith while sitting around their campfire at night. Their understanding of the meaning of life is expressed through recognisable literary forms, the aim of which is not to give a scientific explanation for the origin of life. The purpose is much more theological and philosophical. It's not asking the question about how the world came into being. It's not preoccupied with the scientific process and, in any event, couldn't have come to any conclusions on that score without the complex scientific instruments we have now. Even then, we don't yet know all there is to be known. Their reflection was asking the 'meaning' question, why did the world come into being and why did things go so wrong, evidenced by the suffering of the world, after the wonderful Eden experience where the symbolic representatives of humanity, Adam and Eve, became unfaithful to who they were – persons-in-relationship with God, themselves, others and nature? It's the cry of every generation to find the answer to the cruelty of death, suffering and the contradictions of the heart. They had an awareness of the heart's dis-ease while longing for that elusive healing balm. The Genesis narrative conveys Jewish faith. The narrative draws its own conclusions. God and God's creation are good and purposeful. God invites us into friendship with him so that we will find fulfilment and be who God meant us to be. God wants us to enjoy responsibly the gifts he has made possible.

Then, through a clear and clever narrative we are shown how humans, through the personae of Adam and Eve, rejected their creaturely, dependent status by picking the forbidden fruit from the tree of knowledge. Such an action expressed their desire to be at least equal to God. Their failure to embrace their existential reality brought about their own downfall. They refused to take seriously the word of God, uttered for their well-being and fulfilment. They rejected the God part of a person-in-relationship (God, themselves, others and planet) which, by its very nature, could only fracture them as human beings. They did intense damage to themselves, causing a deep 'spirit-wound' that they wouldn't be able to mend by themselves. As wounded persons, the negative impacts of their 'spirit-wound' rubbed off on others and, as it happened, all too soon. Adam and Eve's 'spirit-wound' quickly translated into 'sin at the door like a crouching beast hungering for you' (Genesis 4:7). This negative force, which their action unleashed, is like the air we breathe, and the next victim of this toxicity is their son Cain, who kills his brother Abel. It can only get worse! They experienced a most bitter and sorrowful family bereavement. Did Adam and Eve blame themselves for being so short-sighted and greedy? Did they notice how their self-inflicted 'spirit-wound' had opened a can of worms? Denying any part of our identity can only inflict a wound on the spirit. It's therefore important to be spiritually aware of our whole selves. We're not self-contained compartmentalised parts. Psychosomatic illnesses confirm that. My running to the bathroom before giving the best man's speech may be caused by my anxiety, which is in overdrive and finds physical expression. Each part of us, spiritual and material, emotional and physical, is related to the whole. The symbolic characters, Adam and Eve, bit off more than they could chew, to their cost. After being found out by God, they went into hiding from the person who loved them most. They rejected the person who could heal them.

The Bible concerns itself with meaningful interpretation while science concerns itself with the mechanics of the origin of the universe. Just as Adam and Eve complemented one another, so too science and faith complement one another. Contrary to popular opinion, science and biblical faith are not in competition, they are compatible companions, science and meaning. A quick Google search will reveal a long list of priest-scientists, many of them still famous. They include Jesuit past pupil Fr Georges Lemaître, who proposed the 'Big Bang' theory about the origin of the universe. If we look at the contribution of these priest-scientists, each added building blocks to our contemporary understanding of science. Many of them were Jesuits debunking any notion that science and religion are incompatible.

A pivotal event in the Old Testament is the great narrative of the crossing of the Reed Sea (often referred to as the Red Sea). The Egyptians are in hot pursuit of the Jews as they escape from slavery. It looks like the Jews are in for it. They will be slaughtered and their corpses will be abandoned in the desert. It's their worst nightmare. The Egyptians are better prepared than the Jewish nomads. They have hundreds of state-of-the-art chariots at their disposal. When inevitable annihilation is staring the Jews in the face, God reassures them that their liberation is imminent. Moses is told to raise his staff and to stretch his hand over the sea. This did the trick. There was a wall of water to the right and to the left and a dry path in between. The Jews managed to get to the other side without being slaughtered.

It's a wonderful narrative that defies credibility. The story is presented as a miraculous escape. However, using the tools of biblical interpretation, we can draw some helpful conclusions. This story is central to the Jewish religion. In the New Testament it becomes a central metaphor. What purpose does this story serve? It's probably based on a historical event or even more than one single event. Yet the story becomes the central Jewish story. It gets embellished, as all good stories do. It adds details to highlight God's providential presence in this event. Why let facts get in the way of a good story? The more important question is what does it all mean?

It's possible to interpret the historical data in a mundane sense. It's quite possible that at this critical moment in Jewish history, there was a predictable confluence of wind, wave and water, not unusual in that part of the world, which made their crossing possible, not unlike a perfect storm where a combination of factors creates a catastrophe, the opposite of crossing the Red Sea but a similar dynamic. The general area where this event may have occurred has its own unique sea, wind and tidal patterns. The Jews were simply in the right place at the right time. Call it coincidence, if you like, but always pay attention to coincidence, because God can be in the thick of it. Another technical term that is used is the word providence, which requires a whole other study. How often do we use the phrase in ordinary situations when we say someone had a miraculous recovery? Or when someone emerges unscathed from a car accident: 'It was a miracle!' What we call miracles may sometimes be a coincidence of events determining an unlikely positive outcome. If person A hadn't been taking the dog for a walk when Person B crashed the car, person B might have died. As luck would have it, Person A was in the right place at the right time and was able to call an ambulance. What appears to be coincidence can sometimes be a sign of God's closeness. The number of steps that preceded this situation for it to happen the way it did is outside our knowledge. Perhaps we can let God enjoy the benefit of the doubt!

The purpose of the Exodus story is to speak about the protective guidance of God experienced through the natural movement of wind, wave and water. We must take the literary details of the story with a grain of salt. We need to recognise the hyperbole of walls of water creating dry ground. The main message of the story is God's intention to show the Egyptians who the God of the Jews is and to demonstrate to the Jews that God is faithful.

Yet there is also an important Jewish principle at play here. In Jewish thinking a loaf of bread, for which thanks is given to God, is the climax of a process, involving different human skills and natural phenomena such as soil, sun and rain, with God as the ultimate cause. When blessing bread the Jews say, 'Blessed be Thou, O Lord our God, King of the Universe, who brings forth bread from the earth.'[43] Wouldn't it be more relevant simply to acknowledge the role of nature and the role of bakers in baking the bread and leave God out? For Jews the answer is clear, 'We bless Him who makes possible both nature and civilisation.'[44] Abraham Heschel continues by asserting that 'even what happens to us as a natural necessity is an act of God'.[45] So, for the Jews who escaped from slavery, thanksgiving was due to God for the favourable confluence of events. If God is the origin of all, then God must be thanked. This is a complex spirituality that doesn't take things for granted and perceives with the eye of the heart the closeness and presence of God. This helps to explain, among many other reasons, why the 'miracle' of the Exodus through the waters of the Reed Sea was such a huge event for the Jews. The coincidence of wind, wave and water was ultimately proof of God's action favouring his people. That was the miracle. Science explains the parting of the waters in one way. Faith interprets the event in another.

By now it should be clear that the Bible is a complex book that requires some minimal tools to decipher the more puzzling narratives because in many parts of the Bible a literal understanding was never intended. One of the New Testament books that gives rise to problems is the final book, known as the Apocalypse of John or the Book of Revelation. This is a particularly challenging book to interpret because it employs the mode of apocalyptic writing, a specific literary genre following recognised literary conventions that allows for grotesque and disturbing imagery, such as 'four animals with many eyes, in front and behind' (Revelation 4:6–7). Not bedtime reading for children! In this type of literature nothing can be taken literally. It's full of complex symbolism, metaphor and allegory. This kind of writing was familiar to Jews and many early Christians, so they understood the conventions of the genre. They knew that apocalyptic literature conveyed its message through a kind of familiar code known to people at the time. It's a bit like George Orwell's novel, *Animal Farm*, a satirical take on Communist Russia, which readers of that time

43. Abraham Joshua Heschel, op. cit., Amazon Kindle edition, p. 63.
44. Ibid.
45. Ibid.

could relate to because they understood the coded message that the satire conveys.

The primary purpose of this kind of genre was to give encouragement and hope to a dispirited people being persecuted for their religious beliefs. Just as there had been persecution during Old Testament times, persecution continued in New Testament times, for example the persecution by the Roman rulers from about CE 37–68. New Testament apocalyptic literature was an acknowledgement of a cosmic battle between the forces of good and evil, as represented by Christ on the one hand, and the Antichrist (the Roman emperor) on the other. Those who were doing the persecuting were the agents of the Antichrist. Apocalyptic writing reassured the persecuted that the victory was already won in the long term and that God would always be with his people. It encouraged an active trust and hope, even against the odds. It was a big ask in the face of the historical facts, but many stepped up to the plate and lost their lives as martyrs.

If we have some basic tools for biblical interpretation, it could help us with some gospel passages where there are apocalyptic echoes that are often taken literally. In Matthew's Gospel, Jesus is reported as saying, 'the sun will be darkened, the moon will lose its brightness, the stars will fall from the sky and the powers of heaven will be shaken' (Matthew 24:29–30). This is an example of apocalyptic discourse whose style is straight from the Old Testament. To appreciate its meaning, we need to read between the lines to get the gist of it. It's like translating a foreign language. If we're aware of that, it takes away the fear that such language can evoke in sensitive souls. Such apocalyptic literature is sometimes hijacked by right-wing fundamentalists who bend truth to suit their agenda. They interpret wars and climate change, with their devastating effects, through the lens of apocalyptic writing and conclude that the end times are near. Yet such an interpretation misses the point. Apocalyptic imagery is also associated with dystopian imagery generated by the devastation caused by war. Such horrific images are referred to as 'apocalyptic' but don't carry the biblical meaning.

The purpose of the Bible is to recount the faith history of the Jewish people and the early Christians. It's a theological interpretation of the events surrounding the historical character of Jesus of Nazareth, whose existence as a historical personage is beyond doubt. No self-respecting scholar denies the existence of the historical Jesus. A principle in biblical composition is the author's flexibility with historicity to frame a theological perspective. There are biblical narratives that seem close enough to the facts, but there are also those whose focus is on interpretive narrative, and biblical narratives will sometimes combine both. The infancy narratives in Luke and Matthew are a creative way of asserting the identity of Jesus as the promised Messiah descended from King David. The narrative employs Old Testament references and Bethlehem, the birthplace of King David, to reinforce the point. When angels get a role in a biblical narrative, it's the author's ways of saying, 'Pay attention. God is at work here.' The role of the angels is to add dramatic effect to reinforce the wonder of what's happening and confirm that God's work is unfolding.

Matthew emphasises how the Old and New Testaments intersect in the person of Jesus. It's likely that historicity is embroidered and embellished to hammer home theological points. Did the narrative unfold exactly as Matthew presents it? Probably not – but that's not the point. The question is how best to convey in narrative form the identity of Jesus. That doesn't undermine the truth about Jesus. If anything, it adds weight to his identity. The birth of Jesus is interpreted in the light of Old Testament faith history by intelligent and conscientious authors who have given much thought to the issues and have done painstaking research. If those who read the Bible are aware that the historical details are embroidered for the purpose of meaning, some of the narratives that defy credulity can be dealt with in a manner that makes sense. The same principle helps us to deal with problems raised by the miracles attributed to Jesus.

The three Gospels of Matthew, Mark and Luke weren't composed until well after the death and resurrection of Jesus. It's generally agreed that Mark's Gospel was the first of the three, written somewhere between CE 64–70, around the time of the Jewish revolution that led to the Romans reducing their sacred Temple in Jerusalem to rubble, and razing to the ground many towns and villages that were thriving during the lifetime of Jesus, similar to the Russian destruction of Ukraine, where President Zelensky has pointed out that villages were wiped off the face of the earth. The Gospels, therefore, were written at a time when many of the familiar geographical places mentioned in them no longer existed or were in ruins. Jews had been forced out of their homes to live elsewhere, those who held precious memories of Jesus, having seen and heard him in the flesh, were now elderly and dying. Back in Rome there was that savage persecution of Christians during the period 64–68 under Emperor Nero, who blamed the Christians for the great fire that caused the destruction of Rome. In those situations, a scapegoat is needed, and what better scapegoat than this new cult of Christianity? It was time for formalising the written traditions because oral traditions couldn't continue for ever. The time was ripe for the New Testament, but the definitive scriptures were written at least thirty years after the event, which allowed time for the community to digest the meaning of their experience of the resurrection.

The four Gospels each had a target audience. Mark's Gospel had Roman Christians in mind. An indication 'of a Roman setting for the Gospel, is Mark's frequent use of Latin loan words, including military terms like legion, praetorium, and centurion and the names of coins. His audience seems to be of mainly Gentile origin since he explains such Jewish customs as ritual washings for readers unfamiliar with them (7:3-4). When he occasionally includes an Aramaic term for vividness, he is careful to provide a translation.[46] Christian communities had already formed and relied heavily on oral traditions about Jesus for information about his life and teachings. Those traditions worked their way into the Gospels. The Gospels also deal with problems and issues that arose in the earliest Christian communities by adapting the Jesus narrative to address concrete issues. There are, therefore, at least three layers – oral traditions, community experience giving rise to questions that needed to be addressed, and the final editing of all the bits and pieces into a coherent whole with a particular target audience in mind. The final edited narrative became a gospel.

The question for the evangelists was the significance of the Jesus event. Their task was the interpretation of factual data. Consequently, the life of Jesus is presented through the interpretive lens of the crucifixion, resurrection, and Old Testament themes about the Messiah. Did those who followed Jesus before the resurrection realise who exactly they were

46. Mary Healy, *The Gospel of Mark*, Ada, MI: Baker Academic, 2008, p. 20.

following? Possibly not. Yet the Gospels occasionally use poetic licence to affirm Messianic identity or other ideas by retrojection. Authors insert dialogue or events based on post-resurrection understanding to support their theological purpose. There is a retrojection of material into the narrative of what could only have been clear after the resurrection. This wasn't an attempt to be misleading or to lie. The purpose of a gospel is to recount a faith story. A gospel is not a history book, but it is influenced by history. Those following Jesus probably didn't grasp the full significance of who he was until after the resurrection. They couldn't have done, because the idea of a future resurrection of Jesus probably was not part of their world-view before the event. The crucifixion itself left them in a pickle, because how could the Messiah have been subject to such an unexpected and humiliating death? Even if they had to tweak their ideas about a Messiah while Jesus was alive, the manner of his death put paid to everything. This death was incomprehensible and, at that point in the story, that was the end for all the protagonists. Time to resurrect their fishing enterprise and return to their permanent and pensionable jobs in the revenue office collecting taxes for a foreign power, having followed a dream that didn't deliver. How foolish they must have felt. The laughing stock of their villages! Peter, James, Andrew and the rest of them a byword for ridicule. That will teach those religious upstarts!

The resurrection is not historically recorded but it is historically experienced, the result of which was the personal and communal transformation of very ordinary, flawed individuals who hadn't anything to gain by trying to fool people. If anything, it was not a good idea to share resurrection experience at that time for fear of ridicule. The authors of the Gospels chose and selected materials to reinforce their theology written from the point of view of the experience that changed everything – the resurrection. And, of course, we mustn't forget St Paul, who was familiar with some of the oral traditions before they found their way into the Gospels.

Target audience, context, literary genre and purpose all help to decipher challenging narratives. If scripture is approached from this point of view, miracle narratives and other issues can make more sense. The point was already raised in Chapter 2 that few people study theology. A decent theology course will include lessons on biblical criticism. It's unfortunate that intelligent people reject their faith based on fanciful biblical stories that defy credibility. A little knowledge of how the Bible works could prevent that. Never was it more urgent to acquire biblical literacy because, as we have seen, it's a complex book that can so easily be misunderstood. Professor of Hebrew Robert Alter sums this up insightfully, when he writes that what 'the Bible offers us is an uneven continuum and a constant interweaving of factual historical detail ... with purely legendary "history"; occasional enigmatic vestiges of mythological lore; etiological stories; archetypal fictions of the founding fathers of the nation; ... and fictionalised versions of known historical figures.[47] Therefore, when interpreting the meaning of biblical narratives, we need to pay attention to the literary mode that parcels the meaning. The multiplicity of literary forms acts as a vehicle for meaning. Jesus himself was the master of fiction par excellence, employing wonderful parables to express the reality of God. He was a natural storyteller, familiar with his target audience, their experience of life and their reference points, and well able to touch their hearts. He had *le mot juste* down to a fine art, guaranteeing his popularity, as those whom he addressed felt he was talking to them as individuals. They noticed that there was something special in the way he spoke, 'as one who had authority' (Matthew 7:29).

On the other hand, it cannot be denied that so much of the Bible has brought great solace to so many. The variety of narratives, even without biblical literacy, has struck a chord. It's not surprising that the parables of Jesus find a home in the hearts of so many people. The parable of the Prodigal Son is a case in point. We can read that narrative and benefit from it without knowing what a parable is. The Psalms are the staple prayer diet for Christian monasteries and for individuals who pray regularly. The imagery of Psalm 23, 'The Lord is My Shepherd', cannot fail to stir the heart, unless it's made of stone. The narrative of the final hours of Jesus doesn't require biblical literacy to empathise with the self-giving love of Jesus. The resurrection stories inspire hope. However, a minimal background knowledge can enrich the understanding and impact of the narrative. Those who pray the Gospels meditatively and imaginatively often find that the biblical narratives enrich their lives and facilitate a

47. Robert Alter, *The Art of Biblical Narrative*, New York, NY: Basic Books, 2011. Amazon Kindle edition, p. 37.

rich experience of God, deepening their spiritual growth and expressing itself in empathy and solidarity.

There will continue to be unanswered, thorny questions concerning some biblical stories. Often the way in to the answer is asking what the author's purpose was and which literary genre was employed to convey its purpose. It also needs to be remembered that in Catholic theology there is a hierarchy of truths. There are essentials that Christians accept. There are also pious beliefs that have been added on that are less important and dubious. What's most important is to focus on the essentials. Mistaken beliefs and practices had to be corrected. Some early Christians believed that the Second Coming was imminent. Central to Christianity is the identity of Christ. The Bible traces the origin and development of Jewish faith, God's promises and their fulfilment in the New Testament. The New Testament needs to be read in the light of the Old Testament. When confronted with the richness of the Bible, we are bathed in the mystery of God's fidelity and graciousness, the constant reminder that God never gives up on us and, through the delicate interplay of free will, human intransigence, and God's desires, God has managed to fulfil his promises in Jesus.

Bible content	Not a history book – faith story
Bible style	Literary genres – figurative language
Based on history	Meaning of events matters.
Biblical theology	Authors write theological stories.
Two Testaments	Old and New – New completes Old

CHAPTER 4

Mass Is Boring

'Mass is boring' is a common remark. There's some truth to it. A knee-jerk defensive reaction is unhelpful. When a young person, or anybody else, describes their experience of Mass, it's well worth listening, potentially facilitating a productive conversation, the outcome of which may be that Mass is indeed boring! It doesn't have to be that way.

Young people often comment positively on their experience of school Masses that are age appropriate and participative. Students can exercise their roles as Eucharistic ministers, readers and musicians, and perform other services contributing to a sense of ownership. Young people and others can relate to homilies specifically directed to their target audience and employing concrete imagery. It's not surprising that Jesus often chose parables to convey his message through folksy imagery that resonated with the hearts of ordinary people. It's helpful for a celebrant who is not a school chaplain to discuss the homily in advance with the lay chaplain to ensure that the content is appropriate for the context. After all, the school chaplain is the person on the front line and is the best placed to make judgements about what's appropriate for the Mass. Where an effort is made to adapt Mass to a particular target group, it can work, such as family parish Masses, or anniversary Masses for the deceased or married. Masses need preparation, especially the Sunday homily, which could be prepared by interested and well-chosen lay people in association with the homilist. The sharing of ideas can be a fertile bed for creativity. Those in the throes of family life may have catchy images and experiences around which the homily could be structured. Other groups may also have an invaluable input. There is a danger that the celebrant can be a bit too unrealistic and idealistic about family life. At a Sunday Mass, the gospel was about taking up your cross daily. The church was full of young families. The homily was an unrealistic call to do more penance. The homilist didn't acknowledge how parents were already giving themselves 24/7. The Pope himself, on more than one occasion, has been critical of the homily that is too long and abstract.

While Mass can be a positive experience on certain occasions, it can also be boring because it's a poor competitor in an environment where serial stimulation is the only game in town and where, in our search for excitement, we flip from stimulus to stimulus, or channel hop in front of the television. Ritual, by its very nature, lands us in an opposite space. However, it's a helpful exercise for parishes to learn from those who say that Mass is boring. A personal experience of boredom can be interpreted in two ways. Firstly, objectively, the style of celebration may indeed leave a lot to be desired. For the priest it could be a robotic mundane performance without any scintilla of passion or human warmth. The priest himself may be bored and going through the motions or he may be imposing personal quirky devotion on the congregation. The choice of music may leave a lot to desire.

Secondly, boredom is a subjective judgement. There may be something lacking in me that's going to contribute to my boredom. If I don't see the point of Mass or if I really don't know what Mass is about, I'm hardly going to engage on a regular basis. Herein lies the nub of the problem. It's a bit like a person who has no interest in soccer going to a soccer game where they're bored because they're uninterested and disengaged. However, if their son or daughter were playing, it would be a totally different experience. To make something come alive, I need to bring some degree of engagement. An increasing number of nominal Catholics no longer identify with Catholicism. The Christian community asserts that the Eucharist is the 'source and summit of the Christian life' (*Catechism of the Catholic Church*, 1324), a phrase that highlights the pivotal significance of the Eucharist. There's a harmonious interplay between life and ritual. However, fewer and fewer Catholics attend Mass except perhaps for special occasions. This constitutes a difficult challenge as to how we do church. If Christians who still have faith, who are living a good life, don't see the point of regular Eucharist, something is missing.

How to pass on a living faith from one generation to another is a perennial challenge. Some stress the importance of religious literacy over religious experience. The converse is also true. When it comes to the Eucharist and faith in general, both are necessary. It's not a case of either/or, it's both/and. It's essential to have the experience of good Masses, but it's also essential to reflect on what Mass means. Mass combines experience and meaning. For many the meaning of Mass has been lost and the experience is hollow. However, on the other hand, the Eucharist is not a forum for theological snobbery. There are those, with a minimal understanding of the Eucharist, who know they are engaging with a deep mystery beyond their comprehension. They are spiritually sustained by regular, routine ritual that speaks to the heart, encouraging them during the inevitable trials of life. Like the religion model outlined in Chapter 2, for many religion will be very much a matter of the 'heart', and the Mass will fulfil a strongly felt devotional need. On the other hand, there are those for whom an intellectual grasp of what's behind the Eucharist is important before they can commit. They want to know what it's all about and why it's so important. Religious faith is always seeking understanding of itself, and temperament inspires whether we're driven more by 'head' than by 'heart'. Once the 'head' is sorted, the 'heart' fits into place. If I'm happy in my head and heart, then I can commit. However, no one wants to give their heart to a false lover, to something that isn't true. Therefore, for some a theological grasp of what's happening is paramount and will help inspire regular commitment because it makes sense.

In Chapter 3, issues in relation to understanding the Bible were highlighted. We have similar issues when it comes to understanding Mass because of its Jewish roots and the way early Christians applied Jewish theology to understand the meaning of the Eucharist. If we're totally unfamiliar with that background, we may be lost during this ritual. For many contemporary Christians, going to Mass is like going to a foreign land where an incomprehensible language is spoken. The Eucharistic prayers have their own unfamiliar technical terms, which owe their origins to the Old Testament sacrificial rites that few in the pew will have grasped. The 'Lamb of God' metaphor is lost on many, as are so many other terms. The Jewish festival of Passover is the key to understanding.

Many nationalities have festival days to celebrate significant events or people from the past. In the US Independence Day falls on 4 July. In

France there is Bastille Day on 14 July. Ireland celebrates its patron saint on 17 March and its secondary patron on the first Monday in February. Jews celebrate the Passover with a special Seder meal, following specific guidelines. On the night when their escape from Egypt was imminent, Jewish families partook of a meal, which became known as the Passover meal, celebrating their escape from slavery. The contemporary mind often finds ancient ritual practices hard to understand, which is to be expected – someone who came from another planet would find our customs hard to understand. This great escape (Passover), as we saw in Chapter 3, would take the Jews to the Sea of Reeds, where they would manage to outmanoeuvre the Egyptians through God's providence executed through a natural confluence of events that would favour their safe passage. For the Jews the escape from Egypt is of pivotal importance. The celebration lasts for about one week in early spring. The Seder meal celebrating the Passover forms the background for understanding the Last Supper. During his last week on this earth, Jesus celebrated his final Passover meal with his closest companions during the Last Supper.

To appreciate the significance of that final meal we need to think about the vocation of Jesus. Each person in life is given a mission or vocation that is unique to them. The challenge is to listen to our hearts and our heads to discover what that vocation is. Serious reflection facilitates this process. Ignatius of Loyola has guidelines to help us. For most of us it's not going to be too dramatic. We're not going to hear voices. We discover our vocation by paying attention to who we are and what inspires us. Where is our spirituality leading us? What gives us energy, contentment, peace and joy? Many hear the call to parenthood and family life, faithfully living out that vocation in their own unique way. They hope to find a job that matches their talents and puts bread on the table. Others may choose to remain single for a variety of reasons, such as caring for a vulnerable person. Others sense a call to religious life as a sister or a brother or a priest. Others find their call in same-sex partnerships. No one else can live our vocation, it's specific to us, even though it might resemble other people's. We each bring our own unique tone to life which cannot be replicated. There will be only one 'me' on the stage of life. Of all the billions of people living and dead, God does not replicate 'me'. We are part of a profound mystery in the way 'me' came into being. This is well illustrated in a provocative personal story of the theologian Michael Himes. He recounts the journey of a young woman travelling to the US with her female companion. During the sea crossing, the companion went above deck for a breath of fresh air while the other woman stayed below deck to assist an expectant mother. A wave swept over the deck, washing the companion into the sea where she perished. The other woman whose life was saved was Michael Himes's great-grandmother. He made the point that 'trillion upon trillion of circumstances, decisions and twists had to go just right for him to come into existence', implying the mysterious ways that bring a 'me' into the world.[48] What would have happened if his great-grandmother had gone on deck with her companion? Would there have been a Michael Himes?

Like the rest of us, Jesus, during his lifetime, had to discover his vocation – his identity, who he was and what he was being called to. Through prayer, the influence of his parents and family, regular attendance at the local synagogue, his cultural and religious heritage, reflection and other factors, he gradually discovered his role as a call to turn back the tide of alienation and dehumanisation, facilitating the implenetation of God's vision for a broken world. He gave his life in order to be God's instrument for saving us from the grip of our destructive demons, both personal and collective. He saw himself as freeing us from anything getting in the way of God's life within us. In theological language his vocation was to initiate the Kingdom of God, with its characteristics of truth, justice, love and peace and all the other humanising attributes that contribute to a life-giving world. His calling was to bring life to the dead and broken places within us and within the wider community. He went public when he was about thirty years of age. The Gospels record teachings and actions, many of which involve healing broken-hearted people from distress and anxiety of one kind or another and restoring them to their selves, which leads to inner peace, life and hope. These life-giving events were a sign that the world was in the birth pangs of a new order that the resurrection would confirm. The power of evil energy in all its manifestations was being confronted by the person of Jesus. The power of

48. Stephen Miller, *National Catholic Reporter*, 16 June 2022.

'winners' over 'losers' was being undermined. The divisions that excluded people from life's feast were being destroyed. However, what Jesus said and did rubbed too many people up the wrong way, especially the political and religious classes and petty-minded cliques and bureaucrats who felt that their influence was being undermined. It suited the controlling elite to perpetuate a 'winners–losers' world. The last thing they were going to allow was someone tumbling them from the pillar of power and prestige. Then, after the Last Supper, Jesus is arrested for sedition, found guilty on trumped-up charges and sentenced to an incredibly cruel and ignominious death on a cross at the hands of the Romans. From his companions' point of view this wasn't meant to happen. The followers had made a huge mistake. And then the resurrection confuses and changes everything.

Now, the early Christians are left with a problem. If Jesus is the promised Messiah, then why did he die such an embarrassing and humiliating death? How are they going to square this circle? Surely the ignominious death of a common criminal undermines all messianic credibility? Messiahs are supposed to be respectable citizens dying in their beds after a long and fulfilled life of positive leadership. Being crucified like a common criminal doesn't fit the profile.

This is where the Old Testament ideas of sacrifice kick in. Animal sacrifices were a central part of Jewish religious ritual, like other religions at the time. There were strict rules and regulations governing this practice. The idea was that sacrificing an animal according to the correct procedures consolidated the relationship between God and his people. Personal and collective sins were forgiven. Sometimes sacrifices were a way of renewing God's special covenant, God's guarantee of fidelity to his people. However, the image of burnt cadavers heaped high near places of sacrifice does not sit easily with contemporary sensibilities. It's physically repulsive, cruel to animals and mind boggling. It's hard even to think that such a practice was taken for granted and nobody batted an eyelid. It was an accepted part of religious culture and not at all unusual. Even Mary and Joseph engaged in this practice when they went to the Temple in Jerusalem to consecrate the child Jesus to God. The ritual included an offering of either a pair of turtle doves or two young pigeons, which was the obligation for poor people. We have moved beyond all that. God uses the cultural and religious traditions of specific times and gradually leads us forward, in much the same way that a teacher instructs in an age-appropriate way, adapting the material to the class, in the expectation that the students would get a more mature understanding when older.

The Mass is sometimes referred to as a sacrifice, which is sometimes misinterpreted in such a way that God's anger at humankind for its way-wardness could only be placated by Jesus. Therefore, God sent Jesus into the world so that he would sacrifice himself on the cross to make up for our sins. This interpretation is far from the truth and does not conform to the image of God in the New Testament. Sadly, it has found its way into popular piety in different Christian communities. It presents God as some kind of monster.

Jesus was primarily a self-giving man. He embraced his vocation, spending his last three years on the road without a roof over his head, relying on the generosity and support of others. He travelled to the towns and villages with a group of men and women. He could see how his mes-sage was negatively impacting the movers and shakers of the political and religious elite. He was an intelligent, articulate, seriously prayerful and reflective young man, with a preferential option for victims of injustice and exclusion. From preaching a novel, challenging message he must have concluded that some day the tables would turn against him. He was well able to read the signs of the times. He was nobody's fool. He could interpret which way the political and religious wind was blowing. There was already a lot of political tension in the air during his lifetime, and it's not surprising he made his way on to the political and religious watchlist for his activities. He would become the object of a political and religious backlash. That didn't stop him in his tracks. His passionate commitment to his cause, now an inextricable part of his identity, would continue to the end. His spirituality was driven by his commitment to God within the Jewish religious tradition. Then, towards the end of his young life, the storm clouds inevitably began to gather. A dark turbulent horizon beckoned. Rather than run away from the obvious ramifications, he decided to accept the potential consequences of his vocation. He could have run away from it all. He could not run away from himself.

Like others before him, he's now in self-sacrifice mode. No matter what lies ahead, he is not going to relinquish his fidelity to his mission or to God. His identity and his mission are two sides of the same coin. He can't be unfaithful to himself. That doesn't make sense for him. He is sinless because he's unable to make choices that make no sense or compromise his identity. He can't turn his back on God, from whom he received his mission and whose love burns passionately in his heart, inspiring him to stay the course. The intensity of his unique life experience prevents him from turning his back on God. It's a bit like the way it makes no sense to hurt your child, so you don't do it. He makes the choice in favour of the ultimate sacrifice, the voluntary laying down of his life for God and others because it is the right choice to make, not because God is forcing him to. Jesus retains his freedom of choice to the end. He's certain no other choice but to be faithful is possible. When he's praying after the Last Supper, he asks God to prevent the inevitable torture that's about to ensue. He concludes his prayer by confirming that God's will takes priority over all else. Yet God's will in this instance is not that Jesus should suffer and die. There is no preordained script he has to act out of. God's will means doing what is right and proper. Sometimes courageous acts have consequences over which we have no control. The self-sacrifice he makes is voluntarily to give up his life as an act of love. That's the nub of Jesus' sacrifice. He also takes this road because he wants us to be certain about God's love for us, which he spoke about in his parables and discourses and especially through his actions. To give up now would implicitly suggest that he was a fraud, a liar, a false prophet, a coward. His death is the guarantee that what he taught was true. How else could he prove it? This is a far cry from the emphasis on Jesus' bloody suffering sacrifice inspired by Old Testament sacrificial theology. The emphasis on the bloody imagery tends to hide the meaning behind Jesus' self-giving sacrifice. The action of Jesus' giving up his life as an act of love and fidelity is what constitutes the essence of his sacrifice. Outside the context of Jesus' sacrifice, we use the word 'sacrifice' in an ordinary sense, such as when a person goes to great lengths to achieve something good, no matter what challenges are involved: 'She sacrificed her free time to help at the soup kitchen.' Essential to sacrifice is giving up something for the sake of a greater good, something that ordinary people do every day of their lives. This is exactly what Jesus did, but the unfamiliar imagery and metaphors inspired by Old Testament ideas can make the nature of his self-giving hard to grasp. Old Testament theology was an interpretive tool for early Christians who grew up in the Jewish faith tradition.

Maybe with some understanding of the influence of the Old Testament on the New Testament we can make some progress on making Mass that little bit more understandable and less boring, especially when we consider that we're in a sacred space where our lives are touched by the extraordinary self-giving of this man Jesus. This sacred space, with its predictable ritual, is an opportunity to dwell in the mystery of God's narrative of his interaction with the world, and not just with the world in general but with me. Eucharist is a space for paying attention to the story we're already familiar with to allow it to permeate our being. It's not a space for novel stimuli and distraction but for interiority and reflection. It's where heaven and earth intersect. How is this story of extraordinary sacrifice, the story of God, speaking to me today? Am I encouraged? Am I more hopeful? How can I respond? What difference does it make to me, anyway? The experience of being loved calls for reciprocity. Mass is not just a passive act on my part in the expectation of new stimuli. It's steeping myself in the familiarity and predictability of the ritual, which for many of us is hard because we can hardly close our eyes or our mouths for a few seconds at a time or disengage from our mobile phones. We might be missing out.

Paul Durcan's poem 'The 12 O'Clock Mass, Roundstone, County Galway, 28 July 2002'[49] manages to portray an attractive vignette of an ordinary Sunday Mass. It captures the essence of worship. It's the intersection of the human and divine, one complementing the other. The middle-aged priest, wearing his Reeboks, is a sports fanatic wanting to make a quick getaway to a hurling match. He gives a brief homily, asking his Galway congregation to pray for a Clare victory against Galway in the hurling quarter-final! A brave man! The ironic humour is not lost, emphasising the ordinariness and humanity of the situation. 'He whizzed through the Consecration / As if the Consecration was something / That occurs at every moment of the day and night; / As if betrayal and the

49. Paul Durcan, *The Art of Life*, London: Random House UK, 2004. Amazon Kindle edition, p. 61.

overcoming of betrayal / Were an every minute occurrence. / As if the Consecration were the "now" / In the "now" of the Hail Mary prayer.' This description of Eucharistic consecration highlights how ordinary life is constantly blessed and spiritual. The consecration at Mass is the climax of this reality. If the ordinary elements of bread and wine become the conduit for Christ's privileged sacramental presence, then the consecration also affirms that all creation is the conduit of God's presence. Nothing is outside God's orbit. The poet Fanny Howe sums this up well when she writes that the 'eucharistic rite, repeated for centuries, is an account of the cooperation of transcendence with the ordinary'.[50] Durcan's description of the priest whizzing through the consecration manages to capture this reality. His poem also highlights in its own way another of Fanny Howe's observations when she writes that while 'the Eucharist is totally mad in terms of human reason, the ritual has another kind of intelligence, one that manages to be both earthy and cosmological'.[51] Such is the mystery and beauty of Mass using two gifts of nature, wheat and grape transformed into bread and wine through human ingenuity and becoming the privileged presence of Christ. What could be more ordinary and extraordinary? As bread and wine are consecrated, so too humanity is consecrated, an idea expressed by Gerard Manley Hopkins in 'As Kingfishers Catch Fire', when he writes, 'the just man justices; ... / Acts in God's eyes what in God's eye he is – / Christ – for Christ plays in ten thousand places, / Lovely in limbs, and lovely in eyes not his / To the Father through the features of men's faces.'

God is able to contain saints and sinners. After life on earth, betrayal didn't prevent Jesus from making it back to his father with the scars of betrayal disfiguring his broken body. Sunday Mass and daily life are inextricably linked. The consecration affirms God's unwavering faith in us despite our betrayals, which are not held against us. God's faith in us is ratified by the gift of his son, who endured an unjust death rather than give up on us. The consecration recapitulates the dynamics of death and resurrection in its different guises. There's the daily reality of betrayal, dehumanisation and alienation, expressed through behaviours that are

50. Ilya Kaminsky and Katherine Towler, *A God in the House: Poets Talk About Faith*, North Adams, MA: Tupelo Press, 2014, p. 115.
51. Ibid.

the opposite of life. Disturbing images fill our television screens on a daily basis as we witness the sufferings inflicted on others by those whose connection with the human family has been severed and who live in their own dehumanised and alienated bubble. On the other hand, there's the possibility of forgiveness, which culminates in transformation, both personal and collective, rolling away the heavy boulder that imprisons us in ourselves. The resurrection is at work in us when our unhealthy desires, fears, insecurities, angers and inflated egos are rolled away, allowing us to be liberated from our false self. Yet we need help beyond ourselves to roll away the boulder, an idea captured by Ruth Fainlight in her poem 'The Angel' when she writes, 'Sometimes the boulder is rolled away, / but I cannot move it when / I want to. An angel must'.[52] The 'angel' is the divine or human outreach that makes it possible for the boulder to roll away. This reality is affirmed at the Eucharist. When Christian communities speak about 'salvation', they are referring to being saved from all that is personally and collectively destructive, the kiss of death. God wants us to experience the kiss of life so that we are free to be who God wants us to be. Yet the story of Adam and Eve reminds us that we often don't want that freedom. We'd prefer to go our own way and destroy our identity as persons-in-relationship. Rolling away the boulder from the tomb of imprisonment frees us to be ourselves. The resurrection can be compared to an unusually bright spring day when the sun suddenly appears, bringing light and warmth, interrupting the monotony of grey skies. That spring day is a sign of hope. It reminds us of what's to come and affirms that the meteorological conditions are already at work, triggering the summer that will follow spring. The resurrection is already at work and partially fulfilled in this world as we await its fulfilment. When we're in the orbit of solidarity and compassion, it's like the spring day heralding the summer and goodness heralding the completion of resurrection.

At the sign of peace, the celebrant asks the congregation to say to one another, 'You are beautiful', not in the sense of physical beauty but in the sense of that beauty seen only by the eye of the heart, seeing the other person from God's point of view and affirming their sacredness, already confirmed by the consecration. Philosophy reminds us that it's impossible

52. Janet Morley, *The Heart's Time*, London: SPCK, 2011, p. 147.

for God to create evil. Therefore, every individual is an embodiment of beauty, albeit sometimes invisible to the naked eye. 'What's essential is invisible to the eyes.'[53] Eucharist challenges us to open our eyes and, in the words of singer-songwriter Dermot Kennedy, to acknowledge 'there's gold in the dirt / I never took the time to see'.[54] Opening our eyes rolls the stone away from our own dark tombs.

At the conclusion of Mass, the congregation is reminded to 'Go now and enjoy yourselves / For that is what God made you to do – / To go out there and enjoy yourselves.' There is a healthy heartiness about this instruction that affirms the ordinariness and blessing of the material universe. This instruction echoes the sentiments of Ignatius of Loyola, who portrays God as wanting 'to share life and love with us for ever. Our loving response to God's friendship is expressed when we embrace life in all its fullness and goodness.'[55] There is a warm, rustic, down-to-earth glow to this Sunday gathering, where God is down-to-earth, and the congregation is having an 'as-it-is-in-heaven' experience. The sacredness of each person and the routine of daily life are highlighted. The hope of transformation coming from forgiveness is recalled. The light of resurrection dawns like a new day destroying the darkness of night and drawing us into the light. Earth is gathered up into the sphere of the divine, with all its mundane activities, joys and sorrows, sanctity and sinfulness, struggles and strife, as God comes down to earth where nothing or no one is beyond his healing embrace. The effect of such an experience on the speaker and their companion in the poem 'The 12 O'Clock Mass, Roundstone, Co. Galway, 28 July 2022' is 'Both of us smiling, radiant sinners'.[56] The experience has been affirmative and hopeful, encouraging our frail humanity. We need not be imprisoned because we are 'radiant sinners'. The Eucharistic dynamic touching our lives shines out from us. God's grace of transformation is radiated through the community experience, not suddenly and dramatically but gently and warmly. A community has been recharged by the grandeur of God if it is willing to embrace the gift and respond to it.

Consider Salvador Dalí's powerful painting *Christ of St John of the Cross* in Glasgow, which helps to bring this reflection on the Mass to

53. Antoine de St-Exupéry, op. cit.
54. Dermot Kennedy, 'Giants', from *Without Fear*, Island Records 2019.
55. Jim Maher, op. cit., p. 21.
56. Paul Durcan, op. cit.

a conclusion. Its point of view is unusual. We're looking down on the world and looking up to the crucified Christ. In the bottom half of the painting, we see fishermen preparing their nets as a new day dawns. The mountains in the background represent the world. In the upper half of the picture a victorious Christ emerges from the pitch-black darkness of dehumanisation, highlighting that the 'crucifixion is the emblematic affirmation that God is no watcher but a full combatant with us in the battle of being against nonbeing, of existence against nothingness, of life against death'.[57] Death in all its manifestations has been conquered. The suffering of Christ is over. Nails no longer immobilise him on the cross. He emerges through the darkness as the victor. What's significant is that Dalí has managed to suggest a victorious cosmic Christ hovering over the world where heaven and earth intersect and where humanity and divinity are in the same frame, where ordinary life is consecrated. It's a bit like Gerard Manley Hopkins's image, when he writes in 'God's Grandeur', 'Because the Holy Ghost over the bent World broods with warm breast … '. Any barriers between humankind and God have been destroyed so that humanity lives in sacred space on holy ground consecrated again by the resurrected Christ every time a Eucharist takes place. We live under the light of the cross as a new creation invites us out of ourselves. God's fidelity to his promises is guaranteed. However, while the final victory is assured, there are many battles along the way. The guarantee of final victory makes the effort worthwhile.

If we are in an intentional friendship with God, it makes sense to join with a like-minded community to regularly acknowledge and celebrate God's presence and faithful love for us. We may already be doing that through personal prayer. But we are social beings, and we like to have communal celebrations. The Mass is the obvious structure to facilitate a communal celebration where the different threads of life's tapestry, the intersection between heaven and earth, are celebrated. We need communal support and reminders that 'the Consecration' is 'something / That occurs at every moment of the day and night; … / As if the Consecration were the 'now' /In the 'now' of the Hail Mary prayer.'[58] Mass need not be boring, especially if we have a more informed view of what it's about and

57. W. Paul Jones, op. cit., Amazon Kindle edition, p. 415.
58. Paul Durcan, *The Art of Life*, op. cit.

it's up to the community in a parish to work together with the liturgical team responsible for regular Mass. Participation at Mass is a bit like an adult child being present to a bedridden elderly parent who has lost touch with the world. The only gift the adult child can bring is personal presence as a way of acknowledging and being grateful for shared experiences inspired by mutual love. It's not going to be an entertaining or stimulating experience. It's going to be a quiet space of memories and ownership of such a mutually life-enhancing relationship. At Mass we acknowledge and are grateful to a self-giving God who invites us into friendship, the fruit of which is recovering and deepening our identity. Attentive presence is the key to making Mass less boring. And one way to help that process is to study the Sunday readings beforehand so that we can enrich our attentive presence because, as we have seen, the Bible is a complex work of literature, which, like James Joyce's *Ulysses*, needs the help of scholarly annotation.

Mass	Eucharist – thanksgiving
Sacrifice	Jesus' voluntary self-giving
Passover – Seder meal	Jesus is the Lamb of God
Privileged presence – bread, wine	Ordinary as carrier of extraordinary
Bread for the journey	Eucharistic bread is transformative.
New Covenant	God's fidelity assured

CHAPTER 5

Mass Maybe

The earliest New Testament reference we have to the Eucharist is from St Paul. The remaining three references come later and are found in the three synoptic gospels. Paul tells us that what he received from the Lord, he passes on to us. He writes that 'on the same night he was betrayed, the Lord Jesus took some bread, and thanked God for it and broke it, and he said, "This is my body, which is for you"' (1 Corinthians 11:23–24). This suggests that a formula for Eucharistic celebration was already in use before the compilation of the Gospels. During Mass the words are a little different but substantially the same: 'Take this, all of you, and eat of it, for this is my Body, which will be given up for you.' A new meaning was being attributed to the Passover meal.

Jesus employed a Jewish ritual through which to interpret the events that were to unfold. He identified himself with the bread: 'This is my body.' It will be broken and shared. The broken bread anticipates his broken body. When we eat this bread, we are in communion with Christ's presence. This Eucharistic bread is to sustain us on our journey. The communion bread 'is not a prize for the perfect but a powerful medicine and nourishment for the weak.'[59] Sitting down to a meal has a twofold function. There is table fellowship in celebrating ties of kinship, friendship and significant events. Food is also meant to energise us for action. After a long day of a pilgrimage retreat in the mountains, some of the students thought their leader was lost. They considered the situation and concluded that they had better follow him, because he knew where the food was! No food, no energy! It's similar with the Eucharist.

59. Pope Francis, *Evangelii Gaudium: The Joy of the Gospel*, Dublin: Veritas Publications, 2013, p. 31.

The blessing of the wine is also full of significance. 'This cup is the new covenant in my blood' (1 Corinthians 11:25). Jesus identifies himself with the wine. There is bread and wine, now the sacramental body and blood of Jesus. An idiomatic expression in some parts is 'our own flesh and blood'. When we speak of our own flesh and blood, we mean blood relatives. The phrase 'flesh and blood' in this context is a conventional code for 'person'. The body or flesh is animated by life-giving blood. For the Jews, blood represented life. Therefore, Jesus' references to his body and blood, his flesh and blood, acknowledge his personal presence in bread and wine. Bread and wine communicate the Self of Jesus.

This blood is also the 'blood of the eternal covenant'. The term 'covenant' comes from the legal world. It means a pact, a contract, an agreement, an accord. A covenant ties a person to an agreement just as a contract does. When a couple get married, they commit to each other for life. It's a form of contract with privileges and responsibilities. There are Church and state legal requirements to support it. 'An eternal covenant' means a contract is binding forever. There's no getting out of it under any circumstances. The term covenant has many biblical echoes, highlighting God's various covenants with his people. The reference to covenant would have been easily understood by Jesus' followers. They would have eventually understood what his intention and meaning were. All the other covenants between God and man, which often involved sacrificing animals, are now replaced by Jesus' self-giving sacrifice – the voluntary handing over of his life inspired by his fidelity to his mission and love of God. The New Covenant is God's absolute guarantee and promise of unwavering fidelity – God will never give up on us. We may give up on God, but God never gives up on us. Mass, therefore, recalls this encouraging reality of God's commitment to us. It's a good reason to regularly celebrate this reality, the unwavering fidelity of God, even when we feel God's absence more than God's presence. Above the darkest clouds, the sun still shines.

The use of Jewish terminology highlights that Jesus is the Passover lamb. There is a link between the saving blood of the Passover lamb and the Lamb of God. All these overtones would not have been lost on the early Jewish Christians. Jewish theology is applied to the death of Jesus as a way of interpreting the event. This explains why, during Mass, we use the term metaphorically – 'Lamb of God who takes away the sins of the world' – and say 'Behold the Lamb of God'. The death of Jesus is interpreted through the lens of conventional sacrificial rites, which makes it difficult for us living in the twenty-first century to appreciate, as we are so far removed from that religious culture ingrained in faithful Jews. Sacrificial offerings were commonplace events, so woven into the tapestry of Jewish faith that it was like the air the Jews breathed.

The blood that Jesus sheds is for 'the forgiveness' of sins. This calls to mind the Jewish atonement sacrifices, the effect of which was the forgiveness of sins, resulting in a personal and collective reconciliation with God. The people were once again at-one with God. Early Christians saw the death of Jesus as a way of being at-one with God – atonement. If a person is willing to die for us, it affirms that they don't hold our wrongful deeds against us. Our sins are forgiven. Jesus doesn't hold grudges. We welcome the gift of forgiveness and respond with a desire for transformation, a graced and concrete expression of our at-one-ment with God. For this reason, we pray during Mass that we 'may become one body, one spirit in Christ'. Forgiveness, as ordinary human experience highlights, brings its own responsibilities. Being forgiven isn't a passive experience, it demands gratitude that leads to action. Therefore, at Mass we celebrate God's forgiveness in our own lives, while renewing our commitment to forgiving others.

Then a simple word with a complex meaning is introduced. 'Do this as a memorial of me' (1 Corinthians 11:25–26). In memory of the first Christmas, Nativity plays are the order of the day during the Christmas season. Children are usually the actors. They play their roles with great gusto, encouraged by doting parents who hope that their child's performance won't bring shame on the family name, or as has been known to happen, the angels won't get into a fight and punch one another! However, 'memory', as used at Mass, is a technical term without its usual meaning. The technical term for 'memory' is the Greek word '*anamnesis*'. Its meaning is not memory in the sense we're used to. It's a difficult concept for our contemporary minds. It refers to an event in the past that can be remembered or recalled in the ordinary usage of those terms. But there is an added layer. It's understood by the term '*anamnesis*' that the past event is re-presented and effective in the present, facilitating our enjoyment of its benefits. Therefore, when we 'do this in memory' of Jesus, the re-presentation and effect of past events impact us in the present. This way of thinking comes from Jewish theology. Jesus and the apostles were familiar with the idea. When they celebrated the Passover, it was as if they were really immersed in the original event themselves and benefiting from its effects. The Passover customs weren't just a re-enactment, they were the re-presentation of the past inspiring the present. It was as if the contemporary Jew was experiencing the Passover event at first hand. *Anamnesis* is where the past and the present intersect. It's neither solely the past nor solely the present. It's both past and present in a dynamic of mutual complementarity, blessing the present moment. A helpful way to get around this is to conclude that a past event is as effective in the present as it was in the past. When we're at Mass, the reality of Jesus' self-giving life is present now. It's a difficult idea for twenty-first century people, but like all difficult thinking, the most helpful approach is to focus on what makes most sense to us. Sacramental remembrance of Jesus' self-giving love is another reason for regular Eucharist.

Perhaps another way to highlight the meaning of '*anamnesis*' is to think of it in these terms. A group of elderly men gathered together to recall and celebrate a significant school rugby victory in the 1960s, when they were teenagers. Decades had elapsed since then, but when the players gathered together to recall the event, it took on a life of its own. The main characters reverted to type. In their recollection of that famous occasion, it was if they were all togged out, playing for their school on that famous day. An event from the distant past was alive in the present as it was on that original day. '*Anamnesis*' takes on some of these characteristics. It's the 'aliveness' of the death and resurrection of Jesus and the potential spiritual energy that comes from it that makes Mass significant, forming 'radiant sinners'.[60]

A few more points need mention before concluding this difficult section. I'm not convinced that it's particularly helpful for personal piety to get too distracted by how the bread and wine are changed. It's sufficient to acknowledge that the consecrated bread and wine constitute the privileged presence of Jesus, as intended by him against the background of the Jewish understanding of '*anamnesis*' and as understood by the apostles, St Paul and the earliest Christian communities. Receiving this bread and wine facilitates an intimate mutual communion in a particular place and

60. Paul Durcan, op. cit.

time, anticipating the fullness of communion in the world to come where the longings of the heart will be finally fulfilled. Yet some terminology is needed to clarify belief and enable dialogue with others. A term used by Catholic Christians is 'transubstantiation', an idea based on the philosophy of Aristotle, of whom Jesus probably never heard! Jesus and the early Christians knew what he was doing without the help of Aristotle. Jewish philosophy was self-explanatory. The mechanics of the Eucharist can be a red herring deflecting from its real purpose and meaning when taken as a whole. It's not just about presence, which is central, but it's bigger than that. It's also about how we respond to that presence. Focusing on presence alone can contribute to passivity. The bread of life isn't an end in itself. It is the food that sustains us for the work ahead. A religious community was having serious interpersonal difficulties. The leader suggested a community Mass. It was a well-intended way of addressing the issues but was a seriously flawed decision because it treated the Eucharist as a magic wand, forgetting that a pro-active response to Eucharist is required. Focusing more on presence than response belittles the Eucharist.

We also need clarify whether the bread and wine are *symbols* of the real presence. Do they *signify* it or *are* they the real presence? What do the bread and wine become? Gallons of ink have been spilled trying to find terms that would capture the essence of Jesus' presence. An elderly priest of a non-Catholic Christian faith tradition accidentally spilled some consecrated wine on the altar, which upset him deeply. He may not have used the term 'transubstantiation', but it didn't really matter, because he was aware that the physical elements of bread and wine constituted a unique and privileged presence of Jesus, requiring reverence and care. This was clear from the Bible. That was enough for him. Does anything more need to be said? Do Christian churches all have to agree on the same shared formula to understand Christ's Eucharistic presence? These are difficulties that could fill many other books.

Jesus chose bread and wine to carry his presence against the background of his voluntary self-sacrificing death, within a ritual context familiar to his contemporaries. When we receive communion, we welcome the presence of Jesus into our lives, the effect of which is forgiveness of sins. In response we pray for personal and collective transformation and increased gratitude while anticipating the life to come and, at the same time, already partially experiencing that life. The Eucharist affirms the resurrection of Jesus, an event in which we all participate until it is fulfilled in us. We place all those we love, living and dead, under the umbrella of God's care, reassured by the promise of God's unfailing fidelity. We also recognise that receiving communion challenges us, personally and collectively, to be the body of Christ in a dark, wounded world where social and climate injustice prevail among so many other evils causing untold pain and suffering to the human family. Participation in the Eucharist implies a creative response to what's happening in the lived reality of my life. I'm invited, along with everyone else, to embody compassionate solidarity in a world of graced dependence. Without regular Eucharistic nourishment I risk having an anaemic rather than a robust response. Eucharistic participation is a formal ritual renewal of my commitment to follow in the footsteps of all those people who followed the ways of the Lord. It's a bit like the renewal of marriage promises. As we receive the broken bread at the Lord's table, we are invited to continue the experience by breaking bread to sustain our families and communities while contributing to the creation of a hope-filled world as a legacy for our children.

At the Eucharistic table there are no social divisions. Even St Paul had to challenge some communities that were composed of the 'haves' and the 'have nots', which undermined Eucharistic fellowship. All human need is there in search of nourishment. All are welcome. We sit together as the human family without exclusiveness. This banquet mirrors how things are meant to be. All of us, rich and poor, with all our challenges and problems, our pain, sorrows and joys, sit alongside one another, offering each other the embrace of fraternity. It's a tall order! There are many historical incidents of social segregation at Mass. One Irish church, in the nineteenth century, had two entrance doors. The 'Penny Door,' at the side of the church, was nearest to the sanctuary. The main entrance door was at the rear. To gain entrance through the 'Penny Door' a person had to pay, was guaranteed a seat and separation from their poor, ragged neighbours who couldn't afford the entrance fee and were left standing at the back of the church. Business class and economy were in operation before the airlines invented them! Even in the time of St Paul, there were social divisions at the Eucharist. 'Surely you have enough respect for the community of God not to make poor people embarrassed? ... I cannot congratulate you on this' (1 Corinthians 11:22).

On one occasion, there was an impoverished elderly woman from an ethnic minority, shabbily dressed, living in challenging conditions, meditatively fingering the black beads on her rosary, sitting in the queue for confession. She had inherited a deep faith from her community. Her poverty and inferior social status weren't going to prevent her from queuing with the hoi polloi. In her view, the church was not a place for segregation. She was an icon of dependence on God. Her faith was strong. After her confession, she would return to her haunt on the street, begging for a few cents while promising to pray for the donor. She knew she had God's ear. That poor woman knew her need for God's embrace in the misery of her life, but in her material and spiritual poverty, she also knew how her experience of God's embrace kept her going. No one has a monopoly on God's favour. In his inaugural address to the nation, King Charles III referred to the contribution of Prince William and his wife to inspiring the national conversations, by 'helping to bring the marginal to the centre ground'. This is one of the challenges of Eucharistic communion. While we are the apple of God's eye, there is no cheap grace. Grace received invites a response – sometimes costly. God's love brings security, privileges and responsibilities. There is no place for the 'Penny Door' at the Eucharist.

If we realise how much we each matter to God and that each one of us has received our own call from God, then we are empowered to achieve our potential. The experience of love transforms us, as ordinary human experience confirms. Meeting the right life partner is often the best thing that happens to us. Our best self is unleashed, and the wounds of the past begin to heal. It's like that between God and ourselves. Human experience confirms countless incidents of troubled people who are transformed by relationships of integrity with those they meet. It obviously works in other relationships as well. It could be argued that if we have no sense of how much we matter to God, Mass won't make too much sense. After all, the Eucharist is an act of thanksgiving. If we have no sense of being recipients through the circumstances of life, then what are we thankful for? A simple exercise to prepare for the Eucharist is to pay attention to what's good in our lives and to refrain from taking things for granted, because the more we take for granted the more our sense of

God is dulled. Most of us have been taught about gratitude since we were knee high. Granny calls to the house. On leaving she shakes our hand and deposits a few euro. We're asked, 'What do you say to Granny?' We say thanks and give Granny a hug. However, like wonder in Chapter 1, the sense of gratitude evaporates over time, replacing gratitude with expectation. I'll expect Granny to put a few euro into the palm of my hand. It can gradually become an entitlement, with no realisation of what sacrifices Granny is making to be so loving to her grandchildren. Eucharistic participation therefore includes not just our thanksgiving, but also the offering of our lives with its joys and sorrows in response to God's generosity. Our self-giving is caught up in Jesus' self-giving.

Gratitude to God can be highlighted through a metaphor. A financially poor young adult wants to go to college. She doesn't have access to finance. A philanthropist comes to the rescue. All expenses are paid up to doctorate level. The student excels herself. Who gets the credit? The student or the philanthropist? Both. The student has used the gift she received in a responsible way to succeed. There is no success without the gift in the first place. Such is life. We receive from God through others and use what we have been given to make the best of it. Therefore, we not only thank others, but we also thank God, the ultimate giver of gifts. This is fundamental to the spirituality of Ignatius of Loyola. We all live in graced dependence.

The account of the Last Supper in John's Gospel is different from those of Mark, Matthew and Luke. The focus is on the washing of the feet, a metaphor for Christ's lifestyle of loving service during his earthly life. When we realise what the washing of the feet signifies for us, we will want to do the same for others. Peter was reluctant to have his feet washed by Jesus until the penny dropped that that's the way God works. God loves us first. We need to welcome healing into the darker recesses of our own lives before we go out healing the world. We need to be freed from the demons that prevent us from practising empathetic solidarity – our fears, our insecurity and other demons. Peter was so independent and proud that he couldn't at first acknowledge his demons to allow Jesus into the fearful chambers of his life. He'd sort himself out in due course. He'd source a self-help book at the local bookshop. It took a personal experience of failure and of God's love and forgiveness to transform him into the man he eventually became, a person willing to lay his life on the line for the Christian cause in the face of persecution. Tradition has it that he was eventually executed for his beliefs by being hung upside down on a cross.

Why couldn't we just practise religion and spirituality in the comfort of our own homes? Why couldn't we just stick to spirituality and avoid the complications of religion? We are persons-in-relationship. No person is an island. We are social animals. We need to belong to community. The impact of Covid-19 highlighted this in dramatic ways as people who were cocooned or had to self-isolate told their sad stories about their intense pain at being cut off from their nearest and dearest. Think of the trouble neighbours and families go to to make sure people don't have to eat their Christmas dinner alone. Our identity includes our link to the community of family and others. This also applies to the community of the baptised. Baptism means connection. We are part of a community that goes beyond our personal boundaries. If we don't accept that we miss the point of Baptism. The big events of life are communally celebrated.

To make Mass more meaningful, we could start by paying attention to our lives, looking out for signs of God's presence. Does this evoke gratitude? There is now no place for offering pigeons, turtle doves or any other kind of animal. Our gratitude is sewn into the tapestry of the Eucharist. We could improve our biblical and religious literacy to help us better understand what Mass is about. If people have the stamina to read James Joyce's *Ulysses*, or some other challenging text, they will have the text in one hand and explanatory notes in the other, helping them to savour the experience, because they will need a lot of help with the allusions. As is the case with the Bible, many of the allusions in *Ulysses* are lost on the average reader. We need to remind ourselves that we're not passive when it comes to being Christian. Once during a theology class, a student put her hand up to ask a question. 'Christianity has now been around for around two thousand years. The world hasn't changed since the time of Jesus. Ugly wars still continue. People starve and go to bed hungry. Those least responsible for climate change suffer the most. Many don't have access to education, a roof over their heads, drinking water and other necessary resources. What difference has Christianity made?' The professor rearranged her glasses, giving herself the opportunity to do some quick thinking. She spoke softly to the student, 'Sylvia, the only way to answer that question is to ask another. How does Christianity affect your life?'

It's presumed that Christians are committed to practising what they preach. But as an influential Jesuit in the area of social justice once remarked, 'If I were to practise everything I preached, I would have nothing left to preach!' However, while many of us try to do our best wherever we find ourselves, experience confirms that we sometimes fall short of the mark for all kinds of reasons. Complete success is not guaranteed in this life. We fail by thoughts, words, deeds, omissions and negative, habitual behaviours that undermine our best intentions. It's ironic that we find ourselves doing the very things we don't want to do. Yet perfection doesn't need to be the enemy of the good. Failure is part of the human condition. It's essential not to be imprisoned by unhealthy guilt or shame. These don't come from a good space. If at least the desire exists to be what I'm meant to be, it's a good start. Regular reflection is a key tool here, following Ignatius's guidelines. Where does my negativity originate? Where does it lead me? What can I do to tame it?

'How has Christianity changed your life?' asked the professor. When people participate at Mass there is a reasonable presumption that such an experience is a desire to welcome God into our space and to respond responsibly to such lavish love. Why else would a person go to the bother of going to Mass? And at least some commitment is better than none, because the Christian community will always be a place for saints and sinners, for people struggling along the way trying to make sense of it all 'with all their problems'.[61] Christian communities are not clubs for the perfect. Some clerical administrators have a 'club' model of church. It's a place where rules and regulations are black and white and if you're not complying, you're not welcome. This contradicts the message of Jesus. It was the experience of having been listened to and loved, warts and all, that brought transformation into lives. Demons are overcome with love. Sadly, this 'club' model of church has turned many people off Christianity. Faith is like a seed that has the capacity to grow to maturity through the seasons. We're all at our own level of faith development and our hope is that it will grow to maturity, but turning away the imperfect impacts negatively on that growth. Making faith judgements about people is a bit arrogant as we have not walked around in their shoes, with their successes, failures and wounds. New ways of being church are necessary.

61. Pope Francis, *The Joy of the Gospel*, op. cit., loc. cit.

Christian communities need to be safe havens for strugglers and stragglers dealing with the complex realities of life. Jesus went in search of those on the margins to bring hope, healing and inclusion. If there is no place in the Christian community for the vulnerable, 'Lord, who shall we go to?' (John 6:68), echoing St Peter's words, albeit in a different context. Spiritual elitism, a form of exclusion, is a contradiction of what a Christian community stands for and everyone 'can share in some way in the life of the church; everyone can be part of the community, nor should the doors of the sacraments be closed for simply any reason.'[62] As a newly ordained priest working in a parish, I noticed that many vulnerable people with serious concerns were calling to speak to a priest. The choice we have now of different support agencies did not exist then. I asked the advice of a wise senior Jesuit who had a lot of pastoral experience. He remarked that if such people are not at home in church, where will they find a home? The point is well made and pretty obvious even in the twenty-first century. The Church is meant to be a haven of support and peace.

And the encouraging fact is that Christianity, despite its obvious institutional failings, is a huge force for good in the world. Ironically, failure can be a blessing, because if we live reflective lives, it can challenge our self-righteousness with a view to doing something concrete to move onwards and upwards, sustained by the hope that the bread from heaven intensifies. It's no accident that at the beginning of Mass we acknowledge that we don't always get it right and that healing and hope are possible. Our personal and collective weaknesses need not be a barrier to joining the 'caravan of solidarity',[63] promoting a 'revolution of tenderness',[64] or what Dorothy Day, would call a 'revolution of the heart which has to start with each one of us'.[65] That's how she lived her life, setting up houses of hospitality, challenging labourers' working conditions and child labour. She also managed to get on the FBI watchlist for her socialist activities. Her personal life, as we saw earlier, had its own serious challenges. Paradoxically, our failures and weaknesses may well be our strengths, as they have the potential to trigger empathetic solidarity and compassion,

---

62. Ibid.
63. Ibid., p. 51.
64. Ibid.
65. Dorothy Day, *Loaves and Fishes: The inspiring story of the Catholic Worker Movement*, New York, NY: Harper and Row, 1963, p. 210.

challenging our complacency and hardness of heart in the knowledge that we are all part of a wounded and bruised humanity and that we don't have it all together all of the time. Our hope is that we are embraced by a victorious, bruised body who empathises with us in our pain, confusion and suffering, and that God, through us, as Simone Weil says, sees the things we see. This is a way of highlighting God's empathy for us. This expectation, celebrated in the Eucharist, gives endless hope to countless people. These last two chapters reinforce the complex and multi-layered reality of the Eucharist, which it is hoped will support reflective presence, acknowledging and thanking God for his goodness and empowering a creative response on our part to advance God's dream for our world.

Old Testament	New Testament
Passover Meal	Last Supper
Sacrificial Passover lamb	Jesus' voluntary self-offering, now Lamb of God
Old Covenant ratified by sacrifice of animals	New and Final Covenant ratified by Jesus' sacrifice
Anamnesis re-presentation – Effects of past event now in present	*Anamnesis* – Jesus' presence in bread and wine. Effects of past now in present
No cheap grace – passive	Costly grace – proactive
Sins forgiven – at-one with God	Sins forgiven – at-one with God
Sign of Jewish religious affiliation	Sign of Christian religious affiliation
Be faithful to God's Covenant	Be faithful to God's Covenant

CHAPTER 6

Jesuits, Spirituality, Religion

The reputation of Catholic Christianity has suffered in recent years for a variety of reasons. However, we're left with a question. Because the Church has so obviously let people down, do we leave, or do we stay? There are compelling reasons on both sides. Expressed more colloquially, it's a matter of deciding to stay inside the tent with the possibility of contributing to change, or staying outside the tent looking in. Christian communities, as discussed in the previous chapter, are made up of saints and sinners. Sinners can do irreparable damage. Do we embrace the reality of failure or allow ourselves to be overwhelmed by it? Good decision-making, according to St Ignatius of Loyola, involves careful attention to the kind of space we're in and how that's inspiring a decision.

This chapter aims to look to the future and consider faith based on the four apostolic preferences of the Jesuit order. The Jesuits are a society of religious men founded in 1540 by the Basque, St Ignatius of Loyola. Many are aware that St Ignatius wrote the *Spiritual Exercises*, a classic work of spirituality that has inspired the lifestyle of the Jesuits and so many others. However, what's called Jesuit spirituality is more accurately termed Ignatian spirituality.

Ignatius came to spirituality by a circuitous route. Up until his late twenties or so, his career trajectory inserted him among the movers and shakers. He was part of the in crowd, enjoying the company of prestigious and influential friends while savouring the benefits of an opulent and lavish lifestyle. Like others at that time, he was a conventional Christian, keeping many of its demands at arms' length. Ignatius came from a rambunctious family in which wild and lecherous parties weren't unusual, especially after victorious local skirmishes where moral caution was thrown to the wind. Even though Christianity was embedded in the family, 'it was that peculiar brand of faith that could willingly shed blood in defence of religion and celebrate the victory with a night of unbridled lechery'.[66] During the first half of his life, Ignatius was no saint. 'Though he was attached to the faith, he lived no wise in conformity with it and did not avoid sin. Rather he was much addicted to gambling and dissolute in his dealings with women, contentious and keen about using the sword.'[67] It is believed that during one of his romantic trysts he fathered a child, who was later adopted. He was even arrested for serious assault but got away with it on dubious legal grounds. A rival in love threatened to kill him. He was given special permission to carry arms to defend himself. We can conclude that Ignatius had a loose connection with religion and a spirituality driven by superficial materialistic values and narcissism. His desire to climb the social and material ladder was his driving force. Yet behind this persona, characterised by an intensity of pride, passion and stubbornness, was an extraordinary spiritual, sensitive and intelligent young man awaiting the intervention of the infamous cannonball, which would set in motion events that would tame his fiery demons, leading him in an unexpected direction that would change the course of history.

On 15 May 1521, while fighting the French against the odds in Pamplona and clinging stubbornly to the hope of victory, Ignatius was struck in the legs by a French cannonball, necessitating a nine-month convalescence at his home in Loyola. Without a racy blockbuster in sight he was bored to tears. The only books available, which were not his cup of tea, included a Life of Christ and books on the saints. These unexpectedly stirred up feelings of doing great things for God, leaving a satisfying afterglow. He would be better than St Dominic or St Francis! He would show them. When he had daydreams about his future career and prospects of romantic liaisons, he felt cold and lethargic in the aftermath. What he thought would excite him left him down. He was introspective enough to notice this phenomenon. This led to further reflection, which reinforced a key insight. Through a careful process of paying attention to

66. W. W. Meissner, *Ignatius of Loyola: The Psychology of a Saint*, New Haven, CT: Yale University Press, 1992, p. 16.
67. Ibid., p. 25.

his moods, feelings and desires, he concluded that God uses these to put us in touch with our truest and best self. This was his epiphany moment, which inspired the rest of his life. Much has been written on this period of life and the dynamics of his conversion from one way of life to another. There is much to be garnered from his experience that is helpful to all of us. There are many people today who have a similar experience and they can identify with the Ignatian dynamic. A person changes career halfway through life to embrace their heart's desire, sometimes involving a loss of income. Yet the affective satisfaction and peace of mind that follows make it priceless.

Based on his new insights, Ignatius's world was turned upside down. We are fortunate that he shared the outcome of his personal deliberations, teaching us a system for self-reflection. He made a choice to leave his home for good and disown all the prestige and trappings of the powerful Loyola family. He set out on the road as an impoverished pilgrim. His family and friends were appalled at his stupidity. How could a man with such ambition, influential social connections, good looks and career potential throw it all aside for a pipe dream? How stupid could you be? How could you give up the prospect of sexual relationships or marriage? What a waste of a man! How could you let your spirituality have such a hold over you? Surely this must be a phase and it will all blow over when he sees sense! The cannonball must have injured more than his legs, more likely his brain!

Having had many colourful experiences along the road, Ignatius eventually ended up as the superior general of the Jesuit Order. The man with a tenuous and selective connection with his childhood religion, who was influenced by a materialistic spirituality, found a warm niche in his Christian religion to which now, as a mature man, he had a renewed attachment and a spirituality inspired by an intense love of God and the sense that 'The world is charged with the grandeur of God. / It will flame out, like shining from shook foil.'[68] After his prolonged conversion experience, he would never experience the world in the same way again. The myopia of his earlier years had given way to seeing things with the 'eye of the heart', which changed everything. He became aware of how

---

68.   Gerard Manley Hopkins, 'God's Grandeur'.

all our experiences have the potential to reveal the divine energy, if only we develop the skill to interpret them.

The spirituality born after his cannonball experience was refined over time deep within the crucible of his crucified spirit and gradually saw the light of day after intense personal struggles that pushed him to the brink of taking his own life. Ignatius systemised his spirituality and passed on helpful guidelines to us. For Ignatius, the key to unlocking the secret of life is to pay attention, because if we do, we will begin to learn how to recognise the signs of God's presence in the very ordinary happenings of life, which, without reflection, could easily pass us by. For Ignatius, seeing with the eye of the heart, penetrating the surface of things, was essential. When we do that, we appreciate the daily miracles hidden by routine. His spirituality is optimistic and upbeat. The world is holy ground, blessed continually by God. As bread and wine are consecrated during Mass, so is the material world, which is the conduit for God's grandeur to 'flame out'. Noticing God's grandeur alters our perspectives. For Ignatius, 'God's grandeur' is a pathway to God, if only, as the poet, Mary Oliver suggests, 'we know how to pay attention,' when we don't 'know exactly what a prayer is'.[69]

Spirituality and religion aren't confined to churches and monasteries. For those who can see, the fingerprints of God are everywhere, exemplified by the way Vincent Van Gogh intuited in the presence of a newborn baby a 'ray from on high', as mentioned in Chapter 1. The bread and butter of spirituality is the ordinary of the everyday. It's here and now, not somewhere else. Yet Ignatius was also a realist and recognised that we all play a part in contributing to the brokenness of the world by our deliberate failures. We don't need reminding of the presence of waywardness. For Ignatius ingratitude and the irresponsible use of God's gifts are the root of all evil, a rejection of our identity as a person-in-relationship.

However, God is not like a judge exacting his pound of flesh in compensation for our wrongdoing. God is more like the concerned parent who wants to bring peace and healing to an anxious and wayward child. This is well illustrated in 'Even-Song', a poem by George Herbert. The speaker is sorry for wasting God's gifts. But he concludes 'Yet still thou

69. Mary Oliver, *New and Selected Poems*, Volume 1, Boston, MA: Beacon Press, 1992, p. 94.

goest on, / And now with darkness closest wearie eye, / Saying to man, It doth suffice: / Henceforth repose; your work is done.' Commenting on this, Mark Oakley remarks that it's as if God is saying, as if to a child who misbehaved, 'It's OK. I know there's been some bad behaviour and that you're worried but get into bed now and sleep well. I love you.'[70] The wonder of God is that we are loved sinners whom God wants to heal, not punish. Ignatius's faith journey can teach us a lot about how to grow our spirituality within a religious tradition. Learning from community wisdom rather than having to reinvent the wheel for ourselves is helpful in our spiritual and religious quest.

The first apostolic preference focuses on the way to God through the Spiritual Exercises and discernment. These 'exercises' are the product of much thought and prayer. To complete the full Spiritual Exercises can take up to a month or longer, depending on the context, involving prolonged daily prayer. Jesuits must complete them at the beginning and at the end of their training. They can also be completed over a period of months against the background of normal life.

The first point to highlight is Ignatius's optimism, as expressed in his 'Principle and Foundation' meditation. 'God wants to share life and love with us for ever. Our loving response to God's friendship is expressed when we embrace life in all its fullness and goodness. We express our gratitude to God by serving others and using the gifts God has given us. We embrace the gifts that help us in our friendship with God and surrender those that don't. All created reality is a gift of God to help us encounter God in this life and the life to come. We respect God's gifts by using them to the best of our abilities and in this way advance God's plan and intention for our world.'[71]

Ignatius came round to this viewpoint by paying attention to his life experiences and reflecting on them. This is one of the principal gifts he has given to us. He repeatedly emphasises the value of reflection and what we can learn from experience. Like Socrates, he has highlighted the importance of examining life to enrich it. If we're struggling with the meaning of life, searching for a spirituality, wondering about church

70. Mark Oakley, *The Collage of God*, London: Darton, Longman and Todd, 2001, p. 32.
71. Jim Maher, op. cit., p.21.

affiliation, thinking about serious decisions, the place to start is to do some serious reflection. This means taking a stand that not everyone is willing to take because it's easier to follow the crowd, avoiding engagement with meaning and direction. On a Quo Vadis pilgrimage retreat, there was a fork on the trail. Some in the group were not paying attention to where they were supposed to be going. They took the wrong turn, only later discovering they were lost. Their hunger quickly facilitated their return to the right path. Life can be like that. We can collectively follow the wrong path by failing to pay attention. It's when we're hungry and lost that we appreciate the importance of the right food for body and spirit. Therefore, checking guideposts and using our intellect is important to ensure we're on the right track. For the Christian, one of the chief guideposts is the Bible. When we know where we want to get to, we can choose the correct path. Building on biblical reflection, the wisdom of Ignatian spirituality suggests that being our best self means that we engage with the reality of our deepest desires about where we want to go in life. If we stop, think and listen to the heart, we'll be surprised at what we find. We'll ask, 'What do I really want out of life?' and 'How best do I achieve my goal?' Ignatius suggests reflective questioning in all areas of life. God gave us feelings, desires, thoughts and intelligence as tools to forge our way forward. For Ignatius that's where God speaks to us. If our rejection of Catholic Christianity is founded on anger, Ignatius will ask us if we are going to handle that anger creatively or if we are going to become a slave to it and let it drive our life. Acting on negative or destructive feelings undermines our true and best self. Destructive anger does not represent what's best in a person, especially when acted out in a passive-aggressive way, leaving everyone else walking on eggshells. Feelings can be like powerful tyrants. Ignatius expierenced this first hand. He almost gave in to his own despair. Yet he found a way to be liberated from the power of destructive feelings. Negative feelings can impact on all areas of life. However, many have found comfort and support in Ignatius's guidelines.

Ignatius can't stress enough the role of reflection. In his Spiritual Exercises he also gives practical and helpful guidelines for making good decisions using our feelings, intelligence and imagination. If we haven't done our homework on fact-finding, we won't make good decisions.

Therefore, before we decide to reject the religion we were brought up in, we need to gather relevant information. Our reason for rejection may be an intellectual misunderstanding. Rejecting the faith of our childhood can be a drip-drip process rather than an informed choice. There's a bit of go with the flow and it just happens. One day we wake up and realise that we haven't been to church for as long as we can remember. Rejection of childhood faith is often a reaction to scandals and ecclesiastical mis-management. For Ignatius, gathering data is essential in the process of decision-making, as is awareness of our blind spots and emotional turbu-lence, which can undermine good decision-making. Often, the heart can take over, undermining the role of the head. My emotional turbulence, my unexamined anger can be in the driving seat, inspiring poor decisions that are not leading to a space of light and life. If that's the case, Ignatius tells me I'm not making the right decision. The best decisions are made in good space. The fruit of a good decision is fundamental contentment, even if the consequences of the decision may be difficult. Yet I'm confi-dent I can live peacefully with it.

Guidelines for interpreting our moods and feeling are also a significant theme in the Spiritual Exercises. Sifting through moods is essential to Ignatius's teaching. As we observed earlier, Ignatius discovered during his convalescence that God speaks to us in the heart through our feel-ings, desires, imagination and thoughts, often expressed through our moods. He has given us tools to interpret which moods are coming from a good space and which are coming from a bad space. This is referred to as 'discernment of spirits', dealt with at greater length in my *Pathways to a Decision*.[72] It's important, if we want to achieve our potential, not to let ourselves be dominated by bad moods that lead to poor action. Ignatius recognises that in order to grow, we must respond positively to our centre of gravity, where the best desires of the heart are inspiring us. Sometimes we need to dig deep down to discover what really matters to us, to meet our best and true self, but the frenetic pace of life often inhibits that process. Therefore, the role of regular reflection for Ignatius cannot be underestimated. The critical questions for Ignatius are, 'Where is this action, this decision, this pattern of life leading me?' 'Am I fol-lowing a path that's life-enhancing or its opposite?' 'Is my life inspired by

72. Jim Maher, op. cit.

generosity, love, patience, joy, good humour, fidelity, self-control, reflective decisions, compassionate solidarity, graced dependence and all those other experiences that are life-enriching?' In thinking about spirituality and religion, Ignatius suggests that these are the kinds of question we might best engage with. Will whatever religion and spirituality I'm drawn to answer these questions affirmatively?

In the Spiritual Exercises Ignatius teaches us different methods of prayer. It's a heartfelt conversation with a friend, using our own words, and going beyond reciting prayers by rote. He gives us a practical prayer called the Examen, a five-step formula focusing on the experiences of the day, identifying where we were touched by God's goodness, where we obscured God's goodness, promoting gratitude and developing strategies to deal with challenges. The Examen is an exercise in learning from daily experience and applying what we've learned. It is an attractive and accessible way of praying that is not difficult to engage with and that has the capacity to grow our spirituality in a life-enriching way while learning to pay attention to our life experience so that we can acknowledge with the 'eye of the heart' that all is consecrated, blessed and gift, and that God gives 'life to all things and makes them holy' (Eucharistic Prayer 3). Ignatius of Loyola lived out of a world-view where he saw God as one labouring 'for me in all creatures' and bestowing 'all blessings and gifts' from above.[73] His vision of the world was inspired by the 'eye of the heart', coming from reflective practice.

Many of us have rejected former models of Catholic Christianity. An older generation remembers the focus on God as a punitive judge and the prevalence of guilt, shame and scrupulosity. Ignatius presents a benign God who, like a loving parent, has our best interests at heart. God is more like the parent whose arms we jump into when we feel under threat, in the certain knowledge that we'll be safe. God is the one who, like a parent, kisses our wounds and makes them better. Those who are fearful of God need to let the fear go to replace it with trust. The generosity and mercy of God can forgive the sins of a person like Rudolf Hoess. Confession, a 'torture chamber'[74] for many, need not be

73. Louis J. Puhl SJ, *The Spiritual Exercises of St. Ignatius*, Chicago, IL: Loyola University Press, 1952, pars 236–7.
74. Pope Francis, *The Joy of the Gospel*, op. cit., p. 30.

if we perceive God as a kind, trustworthy doctor who heals and doesn't upbraid us for our misbehaviour. The past is the past. When we are sorry for wrongdoing, we are not who we were in the past, it's behind us. What matters to God is the content of the heart in the present. When the thief at Calvary asked Jesus to admit him to his kingdom, he wasn't upbraided for past misdeeds, because a new person had emerged from the murkiness of the past, recognising his need for healing and forgiveness. It's as if the thief's crimes were crucified to the cross, as new life emerged ratified by Jesus' promise guaranteeing immediate entrance to Paradise on exhaling his last breath. Committing to Christianity implies at least a minimal awareness of God's outpouring generosity in our own lives. If we can't recognise that foundational and fundamental reality, it's hard to embrace Christianity with an active faith. However, there are those who believe they can approach God only while wearing their Sunday best. They feel they must get their act together first. God comes to us where we're at and we move on from there. If we have to visit a doctor with an embarrassing illness, we must be humble and acknowledge the reality. Then the healing starts.

Spiritual commitment with religion also implies owning our identity. One day we wake up and realise that we're in a world not of our own making. We find ourselves in the world with two parents we didn't choose, in a specific country, in a particular location. Some may feel blessed while others may feel cursed. It's decision time. Do we allow ourselves to be overwhelmed by a reality we're not happy with? Or do we embrace it to make the most of it? Of course, given the enormous pressures some are under, this can be easier said than done and such people will need sensitive support. The problem with Adam and Eve was that they rejected their identity. Living in a world of graced dependence on God overwhelmed them. They were threatened by dependence. They weren't into that. It inhibited their freedom. They took things into their own hands. They ate the fruit of the tree of knowledge in the expectation that such an action would fulfil their hearts' desire. More careful decision-making, along Ignatian lines, would have disabused them of that crazy notion. They had to live with the consequences and so did the rest of us. Graced dependence wasn't half as bad as Adam and Eve had concluded. God really wasn't asking much. He only wanted their friendship. When they stole the fruit and hid, God missed the chat with them in the cool of the evening. Their company meant the world to him. He was hurt when they went into hiding, demonstrating their lack of trust in him. All blessings flow from welcoming God's friendship. The prophet Micah reminds us of God's request: 'only this, to act justly, to love tenderly, and to walk humbly with your God' (Micah 6:8). It's hard to argue with that. A humble person is one who has embraced the reality of their identity as a person-in-relationship living in graced dependence. God is the fountain of all grace that keeps giving, a giving that can never cease. We simply open our hearts to embrace the friendship of friendships. Gerard Manley Hopkins expresses this idea strikingly, employing the metaphor of a fountain, when he writes, 'Thee, God, I come from, to thee go, / All day long I like fountain flow / From thy hand out, swayed about / Mote-like in thy mighty glow' (from 'Thee, God, I come from, to Thee go').

God has a vision for the world. Each person, says Ignatius, plays an essential and unique role in the implementation of that vision. Unlike substitutes in a rugby game, no one else can play our part in the distinctive way that only we can. We may not be certain what our role is, but it's got a lot to do with our temperament and personality. All God wants is for us is to reflect on who we are, on what gives us life, on what we are good at, in which direction we're travelling and how. Our own circumstances determine how best we can contribute to the world. Ignatius again reminds us to reflect from time to time, following the guidelines he gives us for discernment of spirits, decision-making and the Examen prayer. A regular routine of reflection could help prevent common misunderstandings that arise from poor judgement, prejudices, fears, anger, insecurities and the common practice of incorrectly reading one another's mind, such as 'My friend hates me because she didn't turn up at the hurling match.' Her car broke down! Ignatius asks us to presume the best of people until experience determines otherwise. Innocent until proven guilty.

From this viewpoint the Christian life is not focused on what I'm supposed to be avoiding and which penances I'm supposed to be practising. There are already enough of those in our lives without looking for more!

Ignatius makes Christianity an attractive lifelong project, where our very existence matters so much because we're chosen to be instruments of God's plan for the world. And who doesn't want to contribute to making our common home a place where we all feel at home? What we call sins are acts that arise from life-denying behaviours, lack of gratitude, the irresponsible use of what we have been given and prejudices that intensify exclusion and injustice. It's those compromises that become habitual and, if not reflected upon, grow roots. What is technically referred to as 'sin' eventually leads to the death of the spirit, the destruction of our centre of gravity. As so many sins appear under an attractive guise, Ignatius tells us to get out our maps based on the shared wisdom of our Christian community and avoid the pitfalls beforehand by carefully planning for the journey ahead. Forewarned is forearmed. This gets away from the idea of sin as simply breaking rules and focuses more on the values the rules are trying to promote – without getting too obsessive about the rules. We ask ourselves honest questions when making moral choices. Is what I'm about to do consistent with my core values? Does this choice really express my best and truest self? Is this decision an expression of responsible living?

As we might expect, frequent Eucharist was also fundamental to Ignatius's spirituality. Sunday Eucharist is traditionally an identifying mark of Christians, meant to reinforce our faith identity. A regular and responsible Eucharistic schedule is meant to be a support, not a burden. It's the oasis in the desert.

However, Catholic Christianity doesn't do itself any favours in the way it orders people to go to Sunday Mass under pain of eternal damnation! Church leaders and people in the pew are aware of how faith can lose its energy in the absence of regular contact with the Church community. To order people to Sunday Mass under threat of committing a grave sin is unhelpful. The baptised are well able to make their own informed judgements and conscientious decisions. Such a command has caused untold inner torture to sensitive souls who confess that they committed a mortal sin by missing Sunday Mass. Then they add that they were on the flat of their back having a near-death experience in the hospital emergency department! Many people do not pick up the nuances expressed in

Church discipline, and what's meant to be helpful guidance gets caught up in black-and-white thinking that sensitive people can worry about. However, a more nuanced point of view is expressed in *The Joy of the Gospel*, where the Pope reminds us that 'the Church has rules and precepts which may have been quite effective in their time, but no longer have the same usefulness for directing and shaping people's lives'.[75] St Thomas Aquinas 'noted that the precepts subsequently enjoined by the Church should be insisted upon with moderation "so as not to burden the lives of the faithful" and make our religion a form of servitude ... This warning, issued many centuries ago, is most timely today. It ought to be one of the criteria to be taken into account in considering a reform of the Church and her preaching which would enable it to reach everyone.'[76]

What image of God is conveyed through this precept? It's not the God of the New Testament as revealed by Jesus. For Church leaders to think they know the mind of God to the extent that Sunday Mass absentees will separate themselves from God for ever is hard to agree with. Encouraging people to reflect on why a responsible Eucharistic routine is important would be more appropriate. For a person who's in an intentional friendship with God, regular Sunday Eucharist is simply second nature anyway. The definition of 'regular' is an open question, but at least regular enough not to be disconnected from the worshipping community. Experience confirms that if a person doesn't experience regular Eucharist, their Christian identity and affiliation become diluted. It's the shared experience that helps to reinforce Christian identity. Given our human frailty, there may still be times when we need a little encouragement, but certainly not an ecclesiastical nuclear bomb that belongs to another era. We're used to routines and disciplines in other areas of life. If we want to get a place on the hurling team, we accept the challenges of the training regime.

At the spring 2022 meeting of the Irish bishops, it was decided to reintroduce the Sunday obligation, starting on Easter Sunday, reminding us that Mass is 'an essential expression of faith for all'. It's hard to argue with this point of view. Those who have a mature faith get it. However, not everyone is at the same level of faith, and, in any event,

75. Ibid., p. 29.
76. Ibid.

such a message will only be heard by the converted. There are many with a tenuous affiliation to Catholic Christianity, who are living in a competing secular world. Their faith, for a variety of good reasons, is not at the stage where they experience Mass as an essential expression of their faith. In fact for many the essential expression of their faith often involves caring for our common home. As we saw in the introduction, Pope Francis teaches that care for creation is an essential expression of our faith. Both Eucharist and care for our common home therefore are essential expressions of faith. The challenge for Christian educators is to emphasise and clarify the relationship between these two essential expressions of faith, which are two sides of the same coin. This is a difficult task that requires thinking outside the box on the whole issue of Eucharistic celebrations, which are clearly not connecting with a growing number of younger Christians. Growth in faith and its responsibilities is a gradual process and not everyone has exposure to experiences that facilitate that process. This precept needs to be more carefully nuanced and adapted to the complexities of life, especially in a world where many people have to work on Sundays, which is not ideal, and where other positive activities compete for their attention. According to the Catechism, deliberate failure to comply with the Sunday obligation means that a person commits a 'grave sin', putting them at risk of hell, only if the conditions for such a sin are met, something we can't take for granted. In any event, many people, in good conscience, disagree with the precept anyway. It's hard to see how such an authoritarian precept sits easily with a culture of synodality, evangelical outreach and the message of Jesus. The influential German Cardinal Marx, remarked in the context of changing Church teaching on homosexuality that 'Those who threaten homosexuals and anyone else with hell have understood nothing.'[77] The same conclusion could be drawn in relation to the imposition of the Sunday obligation with its sanction of grave sin. Those who do so have understood nothing. The Church can't afford to go backwards to where it was. While regular Sunday Mass is an 'essential expression of faith' for those whose faith has developed, expecting those whose faith hasn't matured enough to fulfil this precept is like asking a First Year to sit the Leaving Certificate exam. Pastoral encouragement,

77. Catholic News Service, in *National Catholic Reporter*, 31 March 2022.

rather than ecclesiastical legalism, would be more appropriate and respectful of people's informed decisions. In any event, in the US, while 'Catholics once regarded Sunday Mass attendance as mandatory under threat of serious sin, this motivation is increasingly ineffective, with 68 percent of Catholics now regarding weekly mass as nonessential to their faith.'[78] Rather than bemoaning this fact, it's more helpful to see it in terms of an opportunity to rethink how Church can be reimagined. It seems pointless to take refuge in the practices of bygone days instead of confronting the contemporary reality with creative responses, including forms of lay ministry and leadership. The Spirit is blowing in the signs of the times for those who have ears to hear. Of course, it could also be argued that perhaps if loosely affiliated Christians were to regularly participate in Sunday worship it could have the potential to grow their faith, but it is, in any event, more welcoming to use the language of invitation rather than the language of sanction and obligation. At a First Communion ceremony, the parish priest, rather than nagging, suggested that those who made their First Communion would return from time to time along with their parents. Seems like a pragmatic and welcoming parish priest.

In the Exercises Ignatius presents us with a positive view of God that is consistent with the image of God represented by Jesus in the Gospels. Ignatius's understanding of God makes Eucharistic celebrations and personal prayer experiences to be sought after. His guidelines on moods, decision-making and assessing the patterns of life in a prayerfully reflective way help us to discern whether we're fooling ourselves or following the way that will lead us to finding God's fulfilment for us. Ignatius has much to teach us about a life-enriching spirituality expressed through religious affiliation. He focuses on the gifts of God and how to embrace them. Sin is the refusal to welcome God's gifts and use them responsibly, including the gifts we may not like, and which challenge us to be more human. A chaplain in a Jesuit comprehensive school, Gráinne Delaney, remarks that she often speaks to students about 'learning about a more grown-up version of God'[79] within the context of Ignatian spirituality.

78. W. Paul Jones, op. cit., p. 28.
79. Alan Hilliard (ed.), *Chaplains: Ministers of Hope*, Dublin: Messenger Publications, 2021, p. 130.

That is precisely what the first Jesuit preference is trying to do. It's a gateway to a more grown-up spiritual and religious experience. The preference challenges us to explore the meaning of our daily experience. It's a way of launching out into the deep rather than anchoring in the shallows. It's a pity to remain in the shallows when the deep has so much more to offer. Ignatian spirituality is a rewarding model for the contemporary religious journey summed up as follows:

I believe in God?	Evidence for and against – an open mind
What is my image of God?	For Ignatius God is giver of gifts.
Do I regularly count my blessings?	Ignatius stresses gratitude.
How do I express my gratitude?	Gratitude expressed through action
To develop friendship with God?	Prayer, reflection, Examen, Gospels
Finding God is goal of Ignatian spirituality	Ignatius not into cult of personality

CHAPTER 7

It's Not Fair

For Ignatius, love of God, or of anyone else for that matter, is down to earth and proved by action. Actions speak louder than words. The second of the four Jesuit preferences is to 'walk with the poor, the outcasts of the world, those whose dignity has been violated, in a mission of reconciliation and justice'. We saw that earlier in John's Gospel; Jesus employs the imagery of the washing of the feet as a model for Christian living. He spent his life metaphorically washing the feet of those in need. It doesn't take rocket science to notice that life is dramatically unfair. Its manifestations are everywhere. Take a walk through any city and pay attention to the homeless sleeping in tents on cold stone pavements during the bleak freezing winter months. Traffickers unscrupulously exploit desperate migrants who are fleeing their countries in the hope of a better life and then finding they're unwelcome. Poverty is endemic. Slavery is booming. Drug addiction is fuelled by big business interests. It's an endless list of man's inhumanity to man. Global lack of justice reflects badly on the whole of humanity. Millions go to bed every night on an empty stomach. Those with addictions wake up every morning to walk the relentless treadmill of intense suffering for yet another day. Life is tough; they no longer have the motivation or energy to change. The miserable life they know is better than the life they don't know. It's an endless cycle of defeated hope. Others look down on them. Many go to bed at night in simple housing, not knowing if flooding, because of global warming, will wash away their meagre accommodation during the night. Many live in the fear that they will have to move from their native village to find a home elsewhere because of the effects of climate change. The world is a very broken place and it's only too easy to shield ourselves from the reality of its brokenness. Unless we experience the world at first hand through the eyes of those who have been left behind, we won't make progress. We can read very fine studies about social and climate injustice, but unless we have experienced its negative impact it will make little sense to us. We can watch heart-wrenching stories on television news, but sitting on our armchairs sanitises sound and smell as we drink another cup of coffee or glass of wine. A flimsy dinghy sinks in the ocean with the loss of lives one day, and the same story is repeated the following day. Despite two world wars and many other armed conflicts during the twentieth century, wars continue to unfold during the twenty-first century as if nothing has been learned from the brutality of previous wars. Who would have thought that Russia would invade Ukraine? Nationalism and xenophobia continue to gain the upper hand. Narcissistic individualism is increasingly prevalent. The idea of empathetic solidarity is falling out of favour. The rich rule the world to serve their own interests, while the rich get richer and the poor get poorer. Many organisations make a positive contribution to supporting those in dire need, and while this is necessary and praiseworthy, it can deflect from the more challenging task of unravelling the unjust systems that give rise to needy people in the first place. As Dorothy Day correctly highlighted in her autobiography, in the Catholic Church there 'was plenty of charity but too little justice'.[80] Fund-raising, involving much generosity and personal sacrifice, is necessary, but it's also essential not to forget that the ultimate goal is to right the injustices that make charitable fundraising necessary in the first instance. Dorothy Day hits the nail on the head when she asks, 'Why was so much done in remedying social evils instead of avoiding them in the first place?'[81] The same question takes on even more urgency today. However, it's also important to emphasise that where people have been deprived of their right to education, housing and healthcare, it has often been church organisations and others who have stepped into the breach to address the issues in the hope that the original injustice will be remedied, and church organisations can then move on to the greater need.

Linked to the second apostolic preference is the fourth one, which is to 'collaborate in the care of our Common Home'. Preferences two and four

80. Dorothy Day, op. cit., p. 150.
81. Ibid., p. 45.

are two sides of the same coin. Climate justice is now the centre of global attention. The planet will no longer be able to sustain itself as heretofore, and those who suffer most because of climate change are least able to influence it. They are usually those who are already poor. Climate change will continue to create millions of refugees escaping drought and famine. The planet itself is threatened. The Jesuit apostolic preferences involve justice issues that are intrinsic to Christianity but have been obscured by less important teachings. On both counts Ignatian reflection can help integrate this into our faith life.

It's easy to be overwhelmed by the state of the world and to feel helpless. There's not much any single individual can do. A starting point is to see how the world works through the eyes of the disadvantaged, the poor, the marginalised and those most impacted by climate change. When leading Sixth-Year Quo Vadis pilgrims on a three-day hike over the mountains, there was an implicit understanding. 'I' am not there yet, until 'we' are all there. No matter how fast or athletic a person was, the pace had to accommodate the weakest. We would often stop to wait for the stragglers who were finding it difficult to climb the steep sections and then continue only after they had recovered. While the stronger may have been frustrated from time to time, there was an invaluable lesson. We walked as a community where people watched out for one another. We weren't in competition. We were in empathetic solidarity. This experience mirrors our better nature.

Being a 'winner', of course, is a gift in so many ways. It's a blessing to have a successful career, influence, a comfortable home and the means of living a quality life, as long as we don't forget empathetic solidarity, social responsibility, and that it's only through graced dependence that we climb the socio-economic and other ladders. No one is a self-made person. Many 'winners' are aware of their responsibilities and are generous with their time, talent and finances in serving the community. However, some 'winners' delude themselves by attributing their success solely to their own efforts, forgetting the essential reality of graced dependence. Who were the countless others in the background giving encouragement and support? Some 'self-made' billionaires choose to ignore the state subsidies that sometimes contributed to their success and their poor treatment of their employees. And in the simplistic 'winners-losers' philosophy, it is believed that the losers get what they deserve. Sadly, while winners are rewarded, the 'losers', otherwise regarded as 'the slothful and incompetent', are relegated 'to a deservedly lowly place'[82] from the winners' perspective. Any scintilla of compassionate empathy is rejected. The prevalence of such an entitled attitude fractures society and retards social progress. Defining 'winners' as the owning class, we can conclude that the 'owning class is committed, with all the ferocity of self-interest, to the principle of socio-economic inequality. This commitment is not merely a matter of greed or malice but a manifestation of a class defending its privileges, that is, a class defending its life.'[83]

The sinful structural inequality of the world contradicts God's vision of human community. It continues to crucify the heart of God. A 2022 Oxfam briefing for Davos 2022, *Inequality Kills*, asserts that inequality contributes to at least 21,000 deaths each day – one person every four seconds. The main contributors to this stark figure are inadequate access to healthcare, gender-based violence, hunger and climate breakdown. Oxfam maintains that these trends can be reversed. It's a hard statistic to accept given the prevalence of extravagantly opulent lifestyles that are self-indulgent and deaf to the needs of others.

While Jesus was dying, absorbing all the pain and injustice of the world, the Gospel states 'There was darkness over all the land' (Matthew 27:45). There are two points here. Political analyst Michael Parenti recalls, in his short memoir, how, when he would fall or hurt himself as a boy, he would run to his Italian grandmother for support. Her reaction was usually the same. 'She would wail and moan along with me, her face contorted, suffering flawlessly as if she were absorbing my pain, making it her own … Who knows? Maybe in some way she actually was absorbing some of the pain. In any case it was always a welcome relief.'[84] Maybe this image is helpful in trying to understand Jesus' empathy for humanity while undergoing such a painful and unjust death, an empathy we're all invited to replicate.

The second point is that it wasn't the Gospel author's intention to give a weather report highlighting how quirky it was to be dark in the middle

82. Michael Parenti, *Power And The Powerless*, New York, NY: St Martin's Press, 1978, p. 86.
83. Ibid., p. 92.
84. Michael Parenti, *Waiting for Yesterday: Pages from a Street Kid's Life*, New York, NY: Bordighera Press, 2013.

of the day. His purpose was to extract meaning from what was happening. The injustice of what was being done to Jesus is described in terms of darkness. The 'winners' were uncomfortable with the threat of this itinerant 'loser' pushing them off their self-serving pyramids of power and prestige. While injustice prevails in all its many forms, the body of Christ still suffers. If one person in a family is suffering, we all suffer. While the brothers and sisters of Jesus suffer, there is darkness over the world, so much so that a question comes to mind. At its most pessimistic, do we live in a world of darkness sometimes interspersed with light or, more optimistically, do we live in a world of light interspersed with darkness?

American poet (not to be confused with the actress) Maggie Smith, in her thought-provoking poem, 'Good Bones', writes, 'The world is at least / fifty percent terrible, and that's a conservative / estimate, though I keep this from my children.' She continues, 'For every loved child, a child broken … / Life is short and the world / is at least half terrible.' She concludes on an optimistic note reminding us that when we put our shoulders to the wheel, 'This place could be beautiful, / right? You could make this place beautiful.'[85]

The importance of justice is central to the Gospel and Ignatius's interpretation of that message is that we're in solidarity with one another. The pursuit of justice and mercy is a priority in the Christian faith tradition, but as experience clearly confirms, it is an uphill struggle, not unlike the myth of Sisyphus. We think we're there, and then another war unravels everything. In George Orwell's novel, *Animal Farm*, there comes a point when the disillusioned animals wonder how their dream of an equal and fair society could have gone so badly wrong. The dejected animals hold a meeting. A faithful, committed and hard-working dray horse called Boxer sums up the reason for the failure of their dream. He says, 'It must be due to some fault in ourselves.'[86] He hits the nail on the head. This 'fault' in Christian terms is called 'original sin', which is the failure to embrace the fact of our identity. We forget about the common good and bully those who want the same as us, so that they can't have what we

85. Maggie Smith, *Good Bones*, North Adams, MA: Tupelo Press, 2017, Amazon Kindle edition, p. 77.
86. George Orwell, *Animal Farm*, London: Penguin Books, 1972 edition (first published 1945), p. 75.

want. We are in relationship to God, others, ourselves and the planet. A distorted 'winners' philosophy rejects this reality, which becomes the root of all evil. The hyper-individualistic mantra, 'what I have, I hold', doesn't serve the global community. It is fundamentally inhuman because it rejects what it is to be human. The way of Christianity is the total opposite and the road to healing. The challenge of spirituality and religion is to reaffirm our identity and take responsibility for it. Experience confirms that many of us want to walk the road of rugged individualism, trampling over the vulnerable who get in the way or slow us down.

In 1963, from his cell in Birmingham city jail, Martin Luther King wrote, 'History is the long and tragic story of the fact that privileged groups seldom give up their privileges voluntarily.'[87] Not much has changed since King wrote these words. Racism, social injustice, xenophobia, exaggerated nationalism and the many other forms of life-denying behaviours abound. Therefore, the urgency of a call to action, demanded by the Gospel, can never be underestimated. Ignatius would share St Paul's view that if any member of the body suffers, the whole body suffers. If any member travelling on life's path is suffering, we are all affected and, again, not to labour the point, 'I' arrive only when 'we' arrive. Yet, as Martin Luther King has taught us, there are always going to be the strongest, who jump ahead first, hogging the hot showers, the best food and the most comfortable bunk in the hostel, without a care in the world for the weak who must make do with cold water, tired food and uncomfortable bunks. Surely, intelligent humans can come up with something fairer that serves us all? Jesus and Ignatius certainly agree. Unless we ask how political and economic decisions impact the poor and the most vulnerable, justice will not prevail. But then, who wants to relinquish power and prestige voluntarily?

Changing the world begins with inner change. Social justice and climate change can come about only if we realise the urgency of the situation. In a 'winners-losers' world we're cocooned and propped up by a consumerism that gives us a false sense of security about the world while we struggle up to the summit of the 'winners' world', only to realise we're not there yet. There's always a bigger and better trophy, a bigger and better summit. The more we climb, the bigger the appetite becomes.

87. Quoted in Michael Parenti, *Power And The Powerless*, op. cit., p. 91.

Why stop here? We're never satisfied. There's plenty more where that came from. Paying attention to the story of a homeless person can teach us a lot and challenge our narrow-mindedness and prejudices. Those who suffer have so much to teach us about life and its injustice, if we only have the ears to hear and the eyes to see, if we're prepared to burst our own prejudicial bubbles, built up over a lifetime, repeating the untruthful and tired mantra: 'They deserve what they get'. We need to look on the world through the eyes of alcohol- and drug-dependent people to get a sense of the burdens they carry. To see how the least vocal and weak 'losers' can be treated by public services is shocking. Assumptions are made based on how they dress or present themselves. It's a case of judging the book by the cover. There is a cohort of people in Ireland and all over the world who have poor literacy skills and lack digital competence through no fault of their own. Yet banks, phone outlets, airlines, public services and so many other agencies hardly cater for them. Such a person walks into a bank and is baffled by the technology and is unable to lodge or withdraw their money. Some customers feel embarrassed and humiliated and, as reported to me, they don't always find staff helpful. Others go to the phone outlet to have something basic and simple rejigged on their phone only to be made feel foolish. There is an unwritten rule that everyone has an email address and a mobile phone. Such insensitivity is inexcusable and socially myopic. There are other fruitful ways of experiencing life apart from the digital rat race. It is encouraging to see that a septuagenarian Spaniard highlighted this issue on 'The Change.org', attracting 65,0000 signatures with the slogan '*Soy mayor, NO idiota*' (I'm a senior, not an idiot). This movement has extended to include people of other age groups who are unable to cope with the digital technologies that many companies use to replace human beings. It's time to reflect on the tyranny of the digital age while acknowledging both its positive and negative impacts. The digitisation of services isolates people, especially those who are vulnerable or living alone, cut off from normal interpersonal contacts, which is not good for society as a whole. How many people complain of never hearing a human voice at the end of a service provider's phone? We remain passive and do nothing to challenge it while the vulnerable suffer in silent loneliness.

If an unkempt person passes out on the street, they must be drunk or drugged. They are side-stepped by passers-by. They don't bother calling an ambulance! That person lying on the street could have had a stroke, heart failure or some other serious illness. However, we (and that includes public services, who can sometimes be quick to judge) jump to conclusions, putting already vulnerable people into neat categories. That person on the street has a partner, children, brothers and sisters, all with their own story. People die on the streets because members of the public fail to act. Am I my brothers'/sisters' keeper?

Storytelling and experience are the best gateways to the heart. They are guaranteed to bring about changed perspectives. Stories, like experience, have a better potential to effect transformation than sterile information, facts, figures or dusty learned tomes occupying spaces in government offices. Stories accommodate different learning styles. They are, therefore, a powerful forces for expanding perceptions.

For most of my life I was tasked with running a social placement outreach programme for Fifth-Year secondary school students, which became a mandatory part of the school curriculum. The aim of the programme was to learn from people whose experience was different from our own. The programme was run in the belief that there is nothing to beat first-hand experience. It was an opportunity to listen to other people's stories on their turf over a few days. Students were not coming into their space as know-all kids from a good school wanting to impose their values. They came with open hands, listening and sharing their experiences. They brought an anxious presence and a listening ear as the comfort zone was stretched. The students were not the ones in control.

At a hostel for the homeless, students were taken aback when a young man told his story. He had gone to the same school. His life had taken a sad and unexpected turn, necessitating a bed in a homeless shelter. How his story touched their hearts! You could read about homeless people but there is no substitute for the human encounter that transforms the heart. A transformed heart has the power to transform society. The lack of decent housing reflects badly on any society and implicitly gives priority to 'winners', especially in the way they can massage the system to their own advantage. Residents of hostels will speak about the fact that a lot of them are dangerous, with many residents feeling threatened as other residents openly take drugs and engage in anti-social behaviour, which vulnerable people find threatening. It's a Catch-22 situation.

Some students spent a few days with marginalised young people and were shocked to the core. All their stereotypical prejudices were challenged and shattered. They learned how parents were in jail, about dysfunctional family relationships and material poverty. They were stunned at what they took for granted and how these young people had to do without. Listening to tragic story after story broadened their horizons and challenged the judgemental attitudes they had inherited from their culture. The storytelling touched their hearts. Going to the young people's neighbourhoods really reinforced their learning. They enjoyed sharing the young people's activities, which facilitated a bonding between the two groups. Without such a placement, neither group would have met each other. It's heartening what a game of pool can do to break down barriers and develop relationships. It might be hoped that for both parties seeds were sown that might produce fruit.

Some students spent a few days in centres for people with special needs. It opened their eyes to the challenges and struggles of families supporting a special needs member. They experienced the self-giving of staff and families, which challenged all they took for granted in their home and school lives. It opened their eyes to the unique and spontaneous personalities of the service-users as they went for walks and shared painting and dance classes with them. Their experience made them aware of how insensitive and disparaging language about some groups could be so hurtful and inappropriate.

Songwriter Phil Coulter has done a great service for parents of special needs children with his soulful song 'Scorn Not His Simplicity', sung by the late Luke Kelly in his inimitable and haunting style (it can be accessed on YouTube). Coulter's son Paul was born with Down Syndrome and the song is a poignant expression of his intense feelings as he came to terms with his son's condition. I recall a parent when they began to realise that their child had a special need about which they were in denial. It was Luke Kelly's wonderful rendition of Coulter's song that kept him going as he struggled to accept his child's condition. As a preparation for our students' placement, the song served as a gateway into some of the special needs issues. Coulter captures the pain of the boy's mother when he writes, 'How she cried tears of happiness / The day the doctor told her it's a boy / Now she cries tears of helplessness / And thinks of all he can't enjoy / Scorn not his simplicity / But rather try to love him all the more / Scorn not his simplicity.'[88] Coulter's suggestion 'to love him all the more' could equally be applied to anyone who's suffering in any way. Those who are hurting need our support. 'Love him all the more' is another way of reinforcing the Gospel message of a preferential option for the poor. Giving priority to loving the vulnerable rightly contradicts the dehumanising philosophy that values a person in terms of their potential for production. Being comes before producing or having – before all else. Where humans are valued only as potential producers, respect for human life is diminished, especially at its beginning and end.

In his poem, 'It Ain't What You Do It's What It Does to You', Simon Armitage describes how he didn't have conventional thrill-seeking experiences such as bumming across America half skint or visiting the Taj Mahal or parachuting from a plane. However, he did live with thieves in Manchester, and mindfully skimmed flat stones across water. Most significant was when he held 'the wobbly head of a boy / at the day centre, and stroked his fat hands'.[89] The impact of such an encounter, which tops the more exciting adventures, is described in the final stanza. 'And I guess that the tightness in the throat / and the tiny cascading sensation / somewhere inside us are both part of that / sense of something else. That feeling, I mean.'[90] He highlights the value and beauty of ordinary things, such as hearing 'each set of ripples' on the water and, more importantly, the superiority of solidarity evoked by contact with the special needs boy and living with thieves in Manchester, echoing his experience as a probation officer.

Other students served on wards for elderly people, organising music, bingo and reading to clients. While massaging the hands of the frail, they listened to their stories and were surprised how rich their experience of life had been and how wrong it was to try to sweep elderly people under the carpet. To discover that one of the residents played a part in

88. Phil Coulter and Bill Martin, 'Scorn Not His Simplicity', Dubliners, 1970.
89. Simon Armitage, in *Paper Aeroplane*, London: Faber & Faber, 2014, p. 6.
90. Ibid.

the Second World War as a medic and another as a bomber pilot really impressed. They were surprised that 'elder abuse' was a reality in families. Of course, there is no place for such 'losers' in a 'winners' world', which has forgotten that we walk the road together and that only when 'I' arrive, 'we' arrive. On occasion parents would question the reason for a student placement. Why did they choose a Jesuit school for their children? Empathetic solidarity is at the heart of what Jesuit schools do. Jesuits fail in their apostolic work if they ignore the plight of the so-called 'losers', who can have more emotional sensitivity than the 'winners'. On one occasion, there was a beautiful non-verbal middle-aged woman with an intellectual disability which necessitated daily support in a centre. A fellow non-verbal service-user was clearly emotionally distraught. The woman noticed and responded by hugging her for some time until she found peace again. It was a reaffirmation of empathetic solidarity and a challenge to the widely held belief that there is only one way of experiencing life to which we must all conform. Obsession with production as the *raison d'être* for human life has clouded our intellect. It's reminiscent of W. H. Auden's enigmatic idea in his poem 'In Memory of W. B. Yeats', where he suggests that 'poetry makes nothing happen'. Consequently, 'it survives in the valley of its making where executives / Would never want to tamper ... '.[91] The implication is that just as business executives would want nothing to do with poetry because of its perceived uselessness, so too society only wants to engage with those who are obviously productive. Therefore, the vulnerable and their needs must be disregarded.

Others had the opportunity to taste what an alcohol addiction programme was like. One sixteen-year-old student returned home after the placement promising never to touch a drop of alcohol again! Listening to the stories of alcohol-dependent young and older adults was shattering. Prejudices and stereotypical images were destroyed. The clients came from all walks of life, including the clergy and the medical profession. Alcohol-dependent people don't have control over their addiction. They would love to be other than they are. Yet expelling demons is hard work, requiring a lot of effort and committed support without any guarantee of success. Facing up squarely to the hurt that alcohol has caused family

91. W. H. Auden, *Collected Poems*, London: Faber & Faber, 1976.

and friends is a gigantic task requiring superhuman courage which can be impossible to sustain. The alcohol-dependent person is suffering in a way few other people suffer. It's hell on earth. It's a vicious circle. There is intense shame and guilt, the feeling that they are no longer lovable. There is the pain of living with the consequences of hurt and pain inflicted on their nearest and dearest. There are false promises, swallowing their pride, begging for 'loans' that are never repaid. If we don't allow ourselves to listen to the story that lies behind the image, our humanity and empathetic solidarity diminish. In the 'winners-losers' world, broken hearts are often unable to find a forgiving and compassionate haven. Instead, they live in hell, the dark abyss of not being able to forgive themselves. Thankfully, in God's compassion and empathy with shattered hearts, by the time they die, they've served their purgatory, as their oppressed spirit is healed by God. Broken hearts are not statistics. They are vulnerable people who have fallen behind and need priority support as a right, not as a begrudging handout. 'There but for the grace of God, go I.' As a society we can't congratulate ourselves on the way we treat the wounded. Handouts, as we saw earlier, do not address the fundamental injustice that makes handouts necessary. They are simply first aid, like a plaster covering a wound without any assessment of the cause of the injury.

One addicted person was living in a dilapidated, dingy, dark and dreary basement flat not fit for human habitation. The landlord was a regular churchgoer. Talking about making a living on the back of the poor! The 'flat' was not fit for a dog! Sex workers and drug addicts roamed the street above. Sadly, the landlord couldn't make the connection between reverence for God and reverence for God's friends. It was okay to receive sacramental communion, but what the landlord failed to grasp was that sacramental communion brings responsibilities expressed through a summons to interpersonal communion with the vulnerable, the broken body of Christ. Communion is not a reward for good behaviour. It is nourishment to become who we are, because becoming who we are is challenging. To be human is always to be becoming. No one is a passive observer at the Lord's table. We're being nourished to get rid of the darkness and to lighten the burden of Christ crucified. At the end of Mass, the question is, 'Where to from here?' The response is to continue loving and serving the Lord in our families and communities according to our own particular circumstances, limitations and responsibilities. Some of the students were welcomed at a local direct provision centre, which taught them so much about the plight of those trying to make a life for themselves in Ireland, and the difficulties they faced. Without their placement, the students and their parents would not have been aware of the challenges involved. A school for the Traveller community welcomed students. It was an opportunity to learn about Traveller culture, which came as a surprise to many and challenged their perceptions.

After the ten-week module, students were required to write a reflection paper indicating what went on in the heart. What did they learn? What were they most surprised by? What did they find most difficult? What was their most memorable moment? How would their experience influence their behaviour in the future? It was gratifying to read the reflection papers, which confirmed that the programme was influential. Most students began their reflection paper by acknowledging how anxious they were before their placement. Some wondered how they might wriggle out of it. They were honest and courageous enough to continue, gradually growing into the experience and coming away wiser than when they started pledging to change their outlook. Some students found their placements difficult if family members were already affected by some of the issues. Those serving at Alzheimer's centres were sometimes reminded of their grannies or grandads, which wasn't easy for them, but they were willing to stay the course and treat the day centre clients as if they were their own family and situate their own family situation in a wider context.

Students also made a verbal presentation in class so that everyone in the class had a sense of everyone else's placement. Of course, the placement was also spoken about with family members and other friends outside the classroom, which helped to promote the culture of placements and outreach. Before going on placement, the various placement issues were addressed in class so that students were thoroughly prepared. They would know what to expect and how to deal with it. Some students made career choices based on their placement. One person became a GP and started an outreach to the poorest of the poor, providing an invaluable and generous service to people who otherwise might not be able to access support, while another worked in the prison service and others worked in a variety of social services. One girl went to live abroad, working with the most challenged young people. Placements were a mutually engaging learning process.

Young people are open-minded and generous before they're tainted by the 'winners-losers' version of the world. They have an instinctive sense of unfairness and a desire to do something. For many young people who have faith, perhaps not in the traditional sense, the performative element supporting justice issues is often a strong point. They may not be going to regular Mass, but they may be serving soup at the local soup kitchen, metaphorically washing the feet of the down-trodden and down-hearted, a way of life modelled by Jesus. They are likely to be involved in LGBTQ+ issues, fund-raising and advocacy groups, and engaging in a host of other community challenges. Spirituality and religion are not pie-in-the-sky experiences. They are part of the bread and butter of everyday experience, but good people sometimes don't make the connection with outreach and spirituality or religion. Getting back to the pilgrim metaphor, the long winding pilgrim path of life involves 'us' trekking as a community to the journey's end in empathetic solidarity and graced dependence, grateful for the way we're often carried by our brothers and sisters, especially when we're struggling with depleted energy and flickering hope in the face of grave injustice or personal challenges.

Boys Town was started in 1918 by Fr Edward Flanagan for boys who needed support. 'He ain't heavy, Father, he's m'brother.' These striking words evoke the spirit of Boys Town, which today includes both boys and girls. The iconic phrase was coined in 1918, when one of the boys who had polio had to wear heavy leg braces. Walking up or down stairs was difficult. A pattern emerged where the older boys would carry him. One day Fr Flanagan asked one of the older boys if he found it difficult, to which he uttered the immortal words, 'He ain't heavy, Father, he's m'brother.' Of course, it could equally be sister. The phrase found its way into a ballad first recorded by Kelly Gordon and popularised by The Hollies and others. Parents are well used to carrying their little one on their shoulders when the child tires on a family walk, and metaphorically carrying them on their shoulders for the rest of their lives. 'He ain't heavy, he's m'brother' highlights the challenge to walk in solidarity with others, especially those who carry heavy burdens.

The planet, like our bodies, is web of interconnections. A stomach-ache will make me anxious and grumpy. A broken leg will prevent me from walking. One part of the body will impact another part. What we do in Western Europe will affect the people in Alaska. If I have set up my garden for a summer barbecue with friends and family, and my next-door neighbour starts setting fire to a pile of weeds and the wind is blowing in my direction, so will the smoke. I confront her and inform her that friends and family are coming over. Her response is, 'It's my garden, and I can do whatever I like in my garden!' As far as she is concerned, what's hers is exclusively hers without any social responsibility or empathetic solidarity. Meanwhile we sit fuming in the garden as the smoke invades our nostrils. Our clothes are smelling of smoke and tears are pouring down our cheeks while we rescue our glasses of wine, spluttering, coughing and wiping the black smutty streaks from our faces. We give up and go indoors to breathe because the asthmatic has an attack and granny's allergy is triggered, resulting in a runny nose, bouts of sneezing, and tear-filled eyes. Blood pressure continues to rise while the neighbour keeps adding fuel to the fire. Flames are rising from the steaks. The smoke billowing into the kitchen sets off the smoke alarm. No one knows where the ladder is, and grandad falls from a chair while silencing the alarm. The ambulance needs to be called for grandad's broken arm. Auntie Patricia, who has been imbibing all day, pours herself another large gin with a drop of tonic and starts singing 'The Foggy Dew', not knowing if it's day or night. The barbecue from hell! This is an image of the world. What an anti-social neighbour can do! And it's not funny!

What I do in my space impacts other people. It's all very well for politicians and multi-national companies to disregard global warming, but, like the neighbour's fire, such irresponsibility has massive repercussions for others. No one owns the world as much as 'winners' would like to believe. The human community is a steward of the world. It's a bit like renting a holiday cottage. We return it the way we got it. We have a responsibility to leave the world in good nick for the next generation. No one has absolute rights within political boundaries. Nations are morally bound to respect other nations and prevent their smoke-filled fires from interfering in the lives of others. What we do on our home patch impacts on others. There is a community in Newtok, Alaska, whose homes are threatened by climate change. It's a small village with about 300 inhabitants. With higher temperatures, the permafrost has begun to thaw, triggering a combination of natural forces leading to flooding and erosion. This is only one example of many that illustrate global interconnectedness. Nature will not continue renewing itself. Animal and bird species will continue to be annihilated. The delicate balance of nature will be destroyed. The global community is at risk. Unless we realise that we have responsibilities to others in our own particular garden, we will annihilate ourselves. Sadly, not only is the planet suffering, it's no coincidence that it's often the poorest who suffer the worst effects of climate change, due to altered meteorological conditions and droughts that lead to famine. Therefore, as already indicated, the second and fourth preferences are two sides of the one coin because their common denominator is justice, social justice and justice for our common home, which we're hoping to leave as a legacy to future generations. They won't have the legacy of a common home unless we take responsibility for stewardship with dramatic urgency – this applies especially to those doing the most destruction.

It's also essential to pay attention to our own personal environment, the bodies we inhabit. I was sharing space on a crowded tram. Next to me was a teenage boy smoking cannabis and giving a lecture to all and sundry on the climate justice meeting he was going to in the city centre. He was passionate and well-informed, but an irony was lost on him. After his speech, I suggested rather mischievously that perhaps he could begin global change by starting with his own body and paying attention to the effects of what he was smoking. Unexpectedly, there was a huge round of applause from the other passengers! Being sensitive to what we eat and drink is essential to our physical and mental health. Huge multi-national industries, contributing to environmental damage, try to persuade us to consume their unhealthy products, which are overloaded with excess sugar and other harmful substances that can cause long-term damage to our bodies. The effects of unhealthy and processed foods on children and adults are well documented. We are what we eat. Taking shortcuts where our diets are concerned is damaging to our health. Unfortunately, healthy eating is a challenge. Not everyone can afford proper nutrition. 'Low-income households can often only afford cheap, concentrated energy from foods full of fat, salt and sugar rather than healthier, more expensive foods such as wholegrains, fish, vegetables and fruit.'[92] It's not surprising that in many countries those with small incomes tend to occupy a disproportionate number of hospital beds. Even in a developed country such as Ireland, many low-income families are forced to choose between nutritious, healthy food and ordinary household expenses. For some, keeping food on the table may mean having to live in a cold house. The choice comes down to eat or heat, especially during times of geopolitical uncertainty.

Christianity has been at the forefront of influencing attitudes to climate change. Respecting the planet is another way of respecting one another and praising God. St Ignatius writes in a meditation, 'Think of God energising, as though He were actually at work, in every created reality, in the sky, in matter, plants and fruits, herds and the like: it is He who creates them and keeps them in being, He who confers life or consciousness, and so on'.[93] The key to Ignatius's understanding, consistent with biblical theology, is the distinction between God and creation. God has given the gift of the world to humankind, who are stewards of creation. It's God who gets the credit. This optimistic attitude is consistent with the purposefulness and goodness of creation as described in the first book of the Bible. Ignatius's reverence for the planet is evident. It is sacred space where God lives and where the grandeur of God is glimpsed and, therefore, is deserving of reverence and respect. God's creation is not an object to be pillaged, abused or destroyed, causing untold damage to nature and people. After all, it is Mother Earth, a nurturing energy. Who would think of deliberately hurting their mother? Unfortunately, it's big corporate multinational enterprises, governments and the wealthiest individuals who do most of the polluting, pillaging and fracking. Between 1990 and 2015 the richest 10 per cent caused 52 per cent of

92. Children's Rights Alliance, *Child Poverty Monitor*, Dublin, 12 July 2022.
93. Louis J. Puhl SJ, *The Spiritual Exercises of St. Ignatius*, Chicago IL: Loyola University Press, 1952, SE, 236.

carbon emissions.[94] We can all play a part by informing ourselves and reflecting on our lifestyles, distinguishing between needs and wants. The way we do things now will no longer be possible in the future. We need to lobby big business and governments while tailoring our lifestyles to accommodate the inevitable adaptations to the reality of climate change. That is not easy for any of us. Things can no longer be as they were. We will need to move to healthier and more sustainable lifestyles for the sake of our children. Lifestyles we take for granted will have to change. This is no longer an option we can procrastinate about in the hope that the problem will go away. It won't. Doing religion, contrary to popular perception, includes looking after ourselves and our planet in a responsible and sensible way while also promoting the well-being of others. The second and fourth preferences can be summed up as follows in the light of St Ignatius's famous saying, 'Love ought to manifest itself in deeds rather than in words',[95] more colloquially expressed as actions speak louder than words, or putting your money where your mouth is. Advancing the cause of social and climate justice is an expression of that love and a concrete step in contributing to a hope-filled future for our young people. It lies at the very heart of spirituality and Christianity. Just as Catholic Christianity in the past was disproportionately preoccupied with sexual morality, Sunday Mass attendance and pious devotions, it now needs to put as much energy and action into social and climate justice as a concrete expression of Gospel values. Such a commitment could become the contemporary Christian badge of honour, along with some regular communal Eucharist to acknowledge the sacredness of the material universe and of each individual, sustained by the creator God, who doesn't despise ordinary matter through which to make himself present and be in solidarity with the broken-hearted, especially during the Eucharistic celebration highlighting God's unwavering faith in us. God's contribution to our lives rather than the mistaken idea of retribution could widen the goalposts of Christianity.

94. Tim Gore, Confronting Carbon Inequality, Oxfam International, 21 September 2020.
95. Ibid., p. 230.

Winners' and losers' world	Others are left to fall behind – not fair
Climate injustice	The earth is mine. I do what I like.
Collective and individual narcissism	I am entitled – I earned it – It's mine.
Spirituality and religion do justice	Justice changes unjust systems.
Learning from others' marginalisation	Melts hearts – promotes solidarity
Journeying on the life path	He ain't heavy, he's m'brother/sister.

CHAPTER 8

Great to Be Young

The third Jesuit preference is to 'accompany the young in the creation of a hope-filled future.' Hope is to be distinguished from wishful thinking, which is passive. Hope is pro-active. John Fitzgerald Kennedy when speaking in Dáil Eireann in June 1963, adapting George Bernard Shaw, said, 'Other people see things and say: "Why?".... But I dream things that never were – and I say: "Why not?"'[96] That is the essence of hope in the context of the third preference. I reimagine a bad situation, asking what can be done to improve it, then I take steps to realise my vision in the expectation that what's hoped for will be fulfilled. I'm moved to act by prudent pragmatism. Hope is incarnated every day in many small ways. Hope is proactively addressing the challenges of life in the belief that we can make matters better. It's the opposite of the cynical view where nothing new under the sun is possible, where we're imprisoned by the status quo. What's the point? Nothing is more urgent in our world than the creation of a hope-filled future. This is at the very heart of Christian spirituality ratified by the resurrection, a sign and promise of what a hope-filled future is in this life and the next. As Seamus Heaney rightly remarks in 'The Cure at Troy', 'History says, Don't hope / On this side of the grave … '.[97] Of course, contributing to the creation of a hope-filled future also presumes the other Jesuit apostolic preferences, reflective living and commitment to social and climate justice. This chapter addresses concerns of young people and steps towards the creation of a hope-filled future.

Youth is a time in life when young adults are searching for meaning, getting to know who they are, finding their place in the world,

96. Dáil Éireann Debates, Friday 28 June 1963, vol. 203, no. 14.
97. Heaney, op. cit., loc. cit.

wondering how best to fulfil their hopes for the future. The passage from childhood to adulthood is often not easy for young people and their parents. There are many challenges and bumps along the road. Many conflicting and contradictory voices compete for attention. There's the conflict between the values at home, the values of peers and those of the wider society. To know the right path is confusing. To be able to follow it is even more daunting. Risking unpopularity and social rejection in pursuit of what they believe is right may leave young people in a very lonely place just at a crucial time when peer support is needed. So many issues seem to end up in the melting pot at the same time. Hormonal changes influencing behaviour and physical growth, anxiety about body image and what's cool or uncool play a big role. The fashion industry holds young people in thrall. The school uniform is simply exchanged for the popular peer brand once school is over for the day. The worry of maintaining friendships and wondering if we're liked or popular is at the forefront of our minds. What are they saying about me behind my back or on social media? Cyber-bullying and other forms of bullying become a concern and sometimes lead to serious and tragic consequences. Video games with violent content can be a source of unease. Concerns about academic ability are reinforced. I discover that I'm not as academic as I thought, and I'm not going to get the points I need to get in to medical school. What's worse, I'm going to disappoint my medical professor mum who seems to love me more for my achievements or for my prowess on the rugby pitch than for who I am. How to deal with sexuality becomes a challenge. Parents are concerned at their children's ease of access to pornography, the confused expectations it raises and how potentially detrimental it can be to their psycho-sexual development.

There is a consensus that pornography fuels male violence against women. At the core of pornography exists the dehumanisation and degradation of a person. This is increasingly embraced in some circles, as the growth in the pornography industry demonstrates, along with the growing number of sexual assaults. This is clearly anti-life; it objectifies and degrades human beings, which is ultimately a denial of human identity expressed through responsible and respectful relationships. Sexual exploitation of any kind contradicts the principle of mutual respect. In an intensely sexualised world, it's a duty to support our children to be responsible and respectful as they negotiate this minefield. It's essential for parents to have open and frank conversations about sexual development rather than leaving it to schools and state-sponsored curricula. It's a challenge to support the psycho-sexual development of young people where dehumanising and degrading sexual behaviours are sometimes tolerated or even expected. A number of high-profile court cases involving sexual crimes have highlighted this. A culture of 'anything goes', where sexual behaviours are concerned, goes against the creation of a hope-filled future for our young people. There are those who suggest that young people should do what young people do. This is fatalistic and unhelpful. One of the ways we grow into maturity is through appropriate discipline and living within reasonable boundaries. To get onto the school soccer team, we're willing to do what's required, and if we're serious about our ambition we don't even think twice about the hurdles involved. We train our pets in basic behaviours, insisting on boundaries. A culture of self-indulgence, either personal or societal, leads to narcissistic hedonism, where the pleasure principle is doing the driving. Competing voices will always generate tensions, which is fine, but getting the balance right is the challenge. Christianity acknowledges the intrinsic goodness of sexuality, but it also recognises that sex, like anger, resentment and fear, can give rise to potent energies that can express themselves in unhelpful ways. Therefore, it invites reflection on strategies to successfully integrate sexuality into a person's life in a way that is authentically human, respectful, responsible and fulfilling. Other related issues also need reflection. What happens if I'm gay? Am I able to come out and own my sexual orientation? Or do I suffer in silence? When it comes to sexual orientation we need to be guided by reputable and responsible scientific conclusions, while not ignoring the biblical context of responsible and respectful relationships guided by our fundamental identity as a person-in-relationship. Biblical authors did not have a contemporary scientific understanding of sexual orientation or other complex sexual issues. If I am having gender identity issues, what do I do? Who can I talk to? Listening to and supporting young people as they integrate their sexuality are essential. Unfortunately, a highly sexualised culture makes young people's growth towards sexual maturity more difficult.

Sadly, some young people witness domestic violence, either men against women or women against men. There are those who are neglected, while others experience sexual, physical or emotional abuse. Others don't know where their next meal is coming from. Preoccupation with social media interactions in place of real interpersonal contact can undermine social and emotional literacy and other interpersonal skills.

Those with special needs, either physical, emotional or intellectual, will be supported during their adolescent years, either in mainstream schooling or in dedicated centres providing supports tailored to their needs. Others won't have that opportunity. Their educational needs are often more complex. All societies must work harder at integrating such young people into the community. Socially and materially marginalised young people at risk tend to get most of the attention while parents of children with special needs must fight hammer and tongs for the welfare of their children. Those parents and their children are often victims of serious injustice. Accompanying the young into a hope-filled future, where hope can sometimes seem elusive, includes giving priority to young people whose disability has caused them to fall behind.

Some young people may be suffering from depression, sometimes undiagnosed as such, anorexia, bulimia, self-harming or other physical and mental health conditions that cause intense anxiety. They may become silent at home, demonstrate angry tantrums and become totally private. Some will discover that formal education is not for them and can't wait to find their way in the world, availing of other possibilities. Parents will remark how, in the later years of school, their children sometimes seem to go into a tunnel where they become little monsters, certainly not the child they gave birth to! Parents worry about their children engaging in risky behaviours. Alcohol, drug and relationship issues are a concern. Thankfully, depending on the supports and opportunities available, many young people come out the other end of this tunnel as balanced, sensible, fun-loving and caring human beings. Of course, not all young people have to face some or any of the preceding challenges. They manage adolescence in their stride. It can also be a period in life when they bring a lot of fun, joy, creativity and many other attributes, brightening up the lives of their families, friends and educators. It can be a wonderful time in life.

Societal changes have influenced family structures. The traditional nuclear family cannot be taken for granted. Blended families are on the increase. Separations occur more often, and single-parent families are more common. Many parents choose not to marry. Same-sex parenting is on the rise. Some parents may not be able to parent due to their own demons over which they have little control. There may be alcohol, drug or gambling issues, or other challenges that inhibit appropriate parenting. Parents may indulge their children as a compensatory measure for not sharing time with them or for other reasons. Parents may prefer to 'befriend' their children instead of 'parenting' them. Consequently, they let their children down by failing to lay down boundaries that are essential to their development. They fail to realise that indulging children is unhelpful. They will set boundaries for their dogs but not their children! Educators confirm that young people are comfortable with boundaries. They dislike the class where anything goes. One of the worst things that can be said about a teacher is that he can't control his class. It unsettles students. Young people need predictability, order and direction. It's easy to get lost on a rugged mountain track on our first outing. Until such time as we're experienced, the advice of those familiar with the terrain is invaluable. When we know the terrain better, we can forge our own path. How we communicate with our young people is important to minimise rebellion. Informed parenting skills are essential.

Many young people, depending on geographical location, are exposed to a world of alienation and dehumanisation where the image of a life-enriching, hope-filled world is replaced by its opposite. They may live in an impoverished or low-income neighbourhood with high crime rates. Neighbours drive flashy cars, wear expensive clothes and flaunt expensive jewellery. It doesn't take long to put two and two together. Young people are recruited into the 'business', to sell drugs, sex and whatever else is the flavour of the month. It doesn't take long for violence and death to result from gangland warfare. In some parts of the world young people are coerced into joining private armies. Underage labour gives rise to ethical issues about where we buy our clothes and other products. Hope is replaced by despair. The temporary elation of the crime boss loses its lustre in a cold, dark jail cell. This topic is intrinsic to social justice, but it's a tough challenge to accompany young people in the creation of a hope-filled future against such a background

Others are able to avail of the opportunity to fit into college life, enjoying a responsible social life, making friends for life. They identify with college societies, many of which support those in need, and engage in college sporting activities. They enjoy their course. Balancing their different commitments is manageable. It's just what they wanted. They are grateful for the way they are academically stretched. They work hard. They have high ambitions and will realise their academic dreams.

As we saw in the previous chapter, the poet Maggie Smith, in her poem 'Good Bones', is ambiguous about our world. On the one hand, she uses the metaphor of a house that's gone to rack and ruin to describe the darkness of this world. On the other hand, she is cautiously optimistic when she remarks to her child, 'You could make this place beautiful.'[98] The house that's destroyed could be restored. The world is full of possibility – a hope-filled ending to her poem. As a mother, she wants to share this hope-filled vision with her child. This is what accompanying the young in the creation of a hope-filled future looks like, the sharing of prudent and pragmatic optimism. A Paddington Bear can easily be purchased. Some bears have a tag attached, saying 'Please take care of this bear. Thank you.' This is a metaphor for young people, who are welcomed into the world. It's as if God attaches the tag, 'Please take care of this child. Thank you.' Being a parent, guardian, educator, or anyone else who supports young people, is a huge privilege, but it is also a massive responsibility. This beautiful new life is totally dependent on others to become who God intended them to be. Nurturing and caring for a child is an act of enormous self-giving, reflecting an intense spirituality, even though we mightn't see it that way. It's the spirituality of Jesus himself, giving one's life for another. It may not literally involve giving up life, but it does involve giving up so much else for the sake of inspiring this child with a hope-filled future. Many parents work so hard at parenting, making multiple sacrifices for the sake of making their children's world a hope-filled place.

A concern that has come to the fore in recent years against the background of youth crime has been the issue of appropriate male role models

98. Maggie Smith, op. cit.

for young men. A paucity of male role models has a negative impact on society as a whole because it can lead to inappropriate and anti-social behaviours expressed through criminality and many other destructive activities. Looking back on his life, Michael Parenti concludes, perhaps with tongue in cheek, that 'females are more highly evolved members of the species than males', and he raises the controversial point that males 'have been the predominant purveyors of war, violence, conquest, rape and sexual abuse, economic rapacity, exploitation, crime, corruption, and political-cultural-religious oppression'.[99] While this caricature may not be fully representative of the truth, it reinforces the fact that there is a male role model issue in some communities, where males abdicate their responsibilities and are more influenced by a culture of a distorted machismo than a culture of care and responsibility.

Sadly, many young people who look up to the crime bosses, usually males, will end up in prison or lose their lives through violence. Criminal exploitation is going in the opposite direction of a hope-filled world. We have seen this in Ireland and many other places. Thankfully many individuals and communities put structures in place to push back the tide of despair. We think of Jesuits like American Greg Boyle, who founded Homeboy Industries, and Peter McVerry in Dublin. When asked for advice on how to bring peace and understanding to troubled youth communities, Boyle says that there 'are no demons here. Just young people, whose burdens are more than they can bear and who are having difficulty imagining a future for themselves. All hands on deck – if you are the proud owner of a pulse – you can be beneficial here.'[100] The point is eloquently reinforced that young people need support in imagining a hope-filled future, especially those who, according to Peter McVerry, have had disastrous childhoods.[101] This is a huge challenge to society.

The influence of role models for good or for ill cannot be underestimated. Our spirituality is embodied in what we do. A parent is worried about her daughter's drinking. It transpires that the daughter lives in a highly alcohol-fuelled home where the family celebrates success and

99. Michael Parenti, *The Culture Struggle*, New York, NY: Seven Stories Press, 2006, p. 58.
100. Gregory Boyle, *Tattoos on the Heart*, New York, NY: Free Press, 2011, unnumbered final page.
101. Peter McVerry SJ, *The Meaning is in the Shadows*, Dublin: Veritas Publications, 2003, pp. 41ff.

drowns its sorrows at alcohol-fuelled events. A father complains that his teenage son doesn't attend Sunday Mass. It turns out that no one in the family ever goes to Mass and prayer in the home is unheard of. Hope is an action word, imagining how a bad situation can be made better. We take appropriate action in the belief that what we do will make a difference. If we think about it, we all have role models who have influenced our lives for good. One urban doctor recalled that his decision to be a general practitioner was primarily influenced by the local GP in the rural area in which he grew up. The GP was an exceptionally skilled doctor with excellent diagnostic skills. He was empathetic and compassionate. He couldn't do enough for his patients, who often needed a listening ear while they shared their stories of rural isolation, troubled relationships and anxieties. The doctor was making hope happen in small ways. Making life decisions based on looking up to role models is not uncommon. How many young people want to be professional soccer or rugby players? Positive role models highlight what is possible. Going to a Jesuit primary and secondary school influenced my choice to become a Jesuit. I experienced at first hand the best and the worst of the Jesuits. Some were inspiring, intelligent, competent, warm-hearted men who could have been successful in other occupations, but they remained faithful to their task of teaching unruly boys, while remaining faithful to their challenging vocation. A teacher being interviewed for a job was asked why she had become a teacher. The answer was definite. She admired one of her teachers at school and wanted to be a similar kind of teacher. A young man on leaving school said he was going to become a plumber because his father was a plumber. Thankfully, the world is full of role models in all walks of life pointing to a hope-filled future. Role-modelling is not drama. It's ordinary, mundane and unpredictably effective. It may only be years later, long after a person is dead, that a person may say that such-and-such a person was the biggest influence in their life. Grannies and granddads are particularly important as role models. Correcting English essays over many years confirms this. Grandparents have a huge capacity for good. But the importance of role models cannot be stressed enough. They often challenge our horizons, perhaps unconsciously, opening new hope-filled ways of seeing the world. To support us in becoming persons of faith, we also need credible role models.

Parents are usually the most significant role models. As a teenager I was dragged by my father either before or after Mass on a Sunday morning to serve breakfast to elderly men in a homeless shelter. My mother conscripted me into helping her to serve 'meals on wheels' to isolated men and women living in Limerick's worst tenements. It was an eye-opener, to say the least. Men and women were living in appalling conditions where they had no access to private sanitary facilities, including running water. There were no baths or showers. They lived in dilapidated former bedrooms with little light, on different floors, which required climbing up the stairs as long as you didn't have painful arthritis, a lung or heart condition, or another debilitating illness. For many, the service was their only point of human contact. On one occasion, my mother welcomed the children of a Traveller woman into our home when their mother was in hospital. It was not without its challenges as the children found themselves in an unfamiliar environment without their mother. A comfortable home couldn't replicate the comfort of the caravan. The importance of such activities was not lost on me, teaching a valuable life lesson at an early age and forcing me to question the failure of social and political structures. Adult children often want to parent and organise family life following the example of their parents. It's ironic and amusing when a mother remarks that she sounds like her own mother when reprimanding her teenage son or daughter! Libby Purves, in *How not to be a Perfect Mother*, challenges some of the idealised notions and expectations of motherhood. As in many other areas of life it's often sufficient to be good enough.

Marybeth Christie Redmond, a writer and a former state representative in Vermont, recalls in an article how the trajectory of her life was turned upside down when she interviewed Archbishop Desmond Tutu as a young journalist. She remarks that she was 'wrestling with questions about my life's purpose and how to serve. This moment in Tutu's presence cast an indelible imprint on my heart and mind: all I could think of was that I wanted to be like this man, living from the deep wellspring of divine soul in everything I did.'[102] After a visit to apartheid South Africa, where she interviewed black farm workers who were victims of inequality

102. *National Catholic Reporter*, 12 February 2022.

and dehumanisation, she concluded that she 'wanted to live a different kind of existence, one that prioritised social justice, mutual relationship with the marginalised, interiority and spiritual growth and a simple lifestyle.'[103] The existence she describes is a powerful image of what a Christian life could look like and what the four Jesuit preferences are promoting. Not all of us have such a dramatic Damascus experience, but her experience powerfully highlights the potential impact of role models who live a robust faith in intelligent conversation with contemporary social and climate justice issues.

Accompanying young people in the creation of a hope-filled future can be challenging. Apart from positive role models, what can be done to promote a hope-filled future for young people? The most obvious response is the opportunity for a young person to be supported in having as good an education and formation as possible, addressing all aspects of the human person – intellectual, social, psychological, physical, spiritual and religious. Retelling the positive events of a community's story is also critical because it reminds us of what we're capable and how to achieve it. It also reinforces the relational aspect of our identity, reminding us that each individual is part of a bigger story.

In former times there used to be the family Rosary. It could be a tense moment, expressing itself in anxious unstoppable giggles! Even if it wasn't always successful, at least it pointed to another dimension of life within the home setting. Perhaps the Ignatian Examen could be a helpful prayer exercise adapted to family situations. Many families have adapted this practice to suit their circumstances. It's especially suited to children as a way of facilitating reflection. Some families will do a short version around the dinner table, with each family member acknowledging and expressing gratitude for the good they experienced during the day. For parents who want to pass on their faith to their children, in addition to a prayer dimension, some tasteful religious iconography is appropriate. For the transmission of faith, the imagination needs the spark of religious imagery. If a family home is bereft of all religious signals an opportunity is missed. Unlike in the past, it's now possible to access a variety of quality religious art, such as very fine icons.

103. Ibid.

On the journey to a hope-filled future, we need to be challenged to broaden our horizons and to assess critically the conventional wisdom so many of us take for granted. The conventional wisdom is often not so wise when put under the reflective microscope where it is observed for what it really is. Unfortunately, both personal and societal biases contribute to making faulty judgements and decisions. Mistaken judgements, influencing how we live, become normative, because they are internalised, like the air we breathe. Those who challenge them, like Socrates, become a threat, a laughing stock or 'old-fashioned' and best sidelined. The 'winners' and 'influencers' want them to be excluded from the conversation, thereby promoting an ideological dictatorship. It's shocking to think that the death penalty is still legitimate in some parts of the world, that the destruction of innocent life is so widely accepted and that so many other dehumanising practices are sanctioned by law. That slavery and apartheid were accepted as a matter of course is an enigma until we realise that societies are ruled by dominant self-serving elites who create structures allowing them to get their own way while strengthening their dominance. Unless we reflect and think for ourselves, others will do our thinking for us, which primarily serves their interests. Unfortunately, we often do not even recognise how manipulated we are by media, culture and popular opinion and we simply parrot and act out the script of our political and cultural masters in the belief that all is for the best. But 'our readiness to accept something as true, or reject it as false, rests less on its argument and evidence and more on how it aligns with the preconceived notions embedded in the dominant culture, assumptions we have internalised due to repeated exposure. In our culture, among mainstream opinion makers, this unanimity of implicit bias is treated as "objectivity".[104] This again highlights the need for a reflective lifestyle that doesn't take the dominant cultural values and beliefs for granted. There are too many cultural enablers and not enough prophets who challenge the status quo, where poverty, inequality and lack of opportunity are all too easily accepted fatalistically. The marketplace of ideas is like a classroom. The more assertive and dominant students hog the discussion, leaving the more vulnerable students, who have much

104. Michael Parenti, *Contrary Notions: The Michael Parenti Reader*, San Francisco, CA: City Lights Books, 2007, p. 33.

to contribute, saying nothing for fear of being belittled. Therefore, the dominant view, even if mistaken due to cognitive or emotional blind spots becomes the only view, and in the process the blind spots are never acknowledged. That's one of the reasons to be in conversations that reflect informed points of view other than our own. Of course, part of that process involves evaluating the source of alternative views.

Agents of socialisation such as the so-called independent media, along with right-wing outlets, tamper with facts to massage their owners' agendas. Newspapers and other media, often run by huge conglomerates, have their own editorial policies to promote the dominant cultural and economic models. In a 'winners-losers' world, the conventional wisdom often asserts that the so-called losers get what they deserve. If young people don't get the untruth of this assertion, their hope-filled future will have time only for 'winners', which is not what life is about. Life is not about climbing the social ladder while name-dropping to remind everyone else how important I am. Since when did my identity become determined by what others think of me? Filling the emptiness inside with more and more consumer pursuits won't bring peace.

Schools and colleges, like the media, convey their own values, attitudes and beliefs, sometimes reinforcing societal divisions. While education is obviously important, not all education is designed to create a hope-filled world. It's designed to propagate the status quo and to reinforce privileged elites following a narrow-minded conventional wisdom often promoted by 'winners'. It contradicts the view that to 'educate is to take a risk and to hold out to the present a hope that can shatter the determinism and fatalism that the selfishness of the strong, the conformism of the weak and the ideology of the utopians would convince us [that it] is the only way forward.'[105] Therefore, we need prophetic educational systems where we challenge unhelpful conventional views while proposing alternatives. It's important for educational structures to aim at inclusiveness. However, it's that commitment to the struggle on the part of educators that makes the difference between a student successfully graduating or prematurely dropping out. There is no such thing as a one-size-fits-all educational system. Educational supports designed for the more

105. Pope Francis, quoted in *The identity of the Catholic School for a Culture of Dialogue*, Vatican City, 2022, 7.

vulnerable will remain a creative challenge, but it's not impossible, as experience confirms. There are different ways of experiencing life. Sadly, our societies have developed tunnel vision where conventional educational attainments are concerned. Success tends to be one-dimensional. Anyone who doesn't fit into the conventional mould sometimes has a problem as far as others are concerned. I suggest it's the other way round. Those who are not academically gifted in the conventional sense have much to teach the rest of us. More reflective living and imaginative thinking would reverse this trend in favour of a more hope-filled future where differences are celebrated and both academic and non-academic talent are acknowledged. In an educational context, 'psychological, social, cultural and religious diversity should not be denied, but rather considered an opportunity and a gift ... diversities related to the presence of particular situations of frailness, affecting cognitive abilities or physical autonomy, should always be recognised and embraced, to prevent them from turning into penalising inequalities.'[106] It's also true to assert that those who 'find themselves in greater difficulties, who are poorer, more fragile or needy, should not be seen as a burden or obstacle, but as the most important students, who should be at the centre of schools' attentions and concerns.'[107] The biggest challenge is how to choreograph these idealistic aspirations within a structure that benefits all. For educational systems this is a concrete way of doing justice and contributing to the creation of a hope-filled world, and an expression of a faith that supports others on life's journey through empathetic solidarity. The international network of Jesuit schools aspires towards these ideals, which are expressed in its ten global identifiers describing what a Jesuit school is about.[108]

We would hope that, as young people develop, they would form a strong and positive self-identity that makes them confident as they face the challenges of life. The content of educational curricula varies. However, it is essential for a young person to be aware of their identity as a person-in-relationship with God, themselves, the human family and the cosmos. This is the reality of everyone's life. Either we embrace

106. Congregation for Catholic Education, *Educating Today and Tomorrow: A Renewing Passion* (*Instrumentum Laboris*), Vatican City, 2014.
107. Ibid., section 5.
108. *Jesuit Schools: A Living Tradition in the 21st Century*, Rome: Jesuit Education Commission, September 2019, p. 18.

that reality responsibly or reject it, with all of the negative consequences for humanity. The extermination camps of the Second World War and other global atrocities didn't occur by chance. There was a perception failure, the populace uncritically nurturing destructive lies spawned by their political leaders in the preceding years, inspiring the unspeakably violent action that was the Second World War, now replicated by Russia's invasion of Ukraine with all its wanton destruction. There was an idea in Nazi Germany that not all were entitled to their fair share of life's banquet. It was only for the so-called strong, and the 'losers' had to fend for themselves. 'Losers', those who were different, Jews, priests, homosexuals, gypsies, foreigners, and so many others by whom people felt threatened, were scapegoated and exterminated. No matter what we do in the challenging work of education and parenting, we fail if we do not highlight that our self-identity is primarily relational, with privileges and responsibilities. Many are aware of their rights, but fewer of their responsibilities. In our fragile common home, the planet that we share, it is a fact of life that there is the 'I' and the 'we,' working in a delicate harmony where interdependence and graced dependence are at the root of our existence. Young people will imitate what they see adults doing. 'Monkey see, monkey do!' Humans are essentially imitators; they do what they see others doing. Observe a child who has just received a toy kitchen set for Christmas – in jig time he's aping his mum or dad, imagining he's cooking a meal. We can never underestimate what we model in accompanying young people in the creation of a hope-filled world, and young people pick up on hypocrisy quickly.

Nurturing young people is a responsible and challenging task. How we parent, how we teach, how we form young people to create a hope-filled world depends to a huge extent on what we do. Adults need to be self-reflective in the Ignatian sense, paying attention to thoughts, desires, feelings and actions. Where am I, as an adult, being led in my own life? What do I really value? Am I open to the possibility of God? Am I inheriting the conventional wisdom of the day without some critical response? As well as my child, am I also 'monkey see, monkey do' where socio-cultural fashions and fads are concerned? Am I buying into the overpowering materialism and the ubiquitous consumerism to bolster my social status? As a family, do we have meals where the phones and other gadgets are switched off? Do we say grace before meals, acknowledging our dependence on God and others? Do we have a model for a family Examen, promoting gratitude to God, acknowledging signs of God's presence, and taking responsibility for our actions? If there are no shared family meals, what's that saying about the value of family communication and other dimensions of reality? Do we model behaviours that highlight for young people the necessity of respect and support for 'losers' or 'scumbags', other ethnic groups? How do we as a family speak about people on the margins? Do we reinforce exclusion by our own behaviour and prejudices? That is one of the reasons why structured experiences, where young people can befriend those whose life experience is different from their own, are essential. Parents are not helping their children or the human community if they object to such experiences. Primary socialisation takes place in the family, while secondary socialisation takes place at school. It can therefore be the case that elements of a school ethos can be overridden by family beliefs, some of which may be uninformed. Parents need to be honest about whether they support a school's ethos. No one ever said that being a Christian trying to shape a hope-filled world was going to be easy. Ignatius of Loyola challenges our prejudices through his decision-making guidelines. He wants us to make good judgements, where our intellectual and emotional biases are put under the microscope. This is part of what it means to be human.

This book has tried to suggest a gateway to spirituality and religion other than the perceived conventional and joyless straitjacket image. It has attempted to alter the focus. Christianity gets a bad press for many good reasons already discussed. It's regarded as a killjoy and out of touch with the real world, which is true in some ways. According to many it's the enemy of sexuality and sensuality. There used to be a hyperbolic mocking understanding of Catholic Christianity. If you took pleasure in something, no matter how innocent, it was sinful! Unfortunately, it's not seen as an experience that is meant to be liberating. Yet that need not be the case if we look at religious experience through the lens of the four Jesuit preferences, which come at religion and spirituality from a liberating angle, following the wisdom of Ignatius of Loyola. It's hard to disagree with them.

The value of transmitting spirituality-with-religion to young people cannot be underestimated. Two Harvard University scientists, Ying

Chen and Tyler VanderWeele have done a considerable amount of research in the US on how religion affects young people and adults. The consensus of their research is that religion is an enormous force for well-being, for physical and mental health. The Harvard scientists did painstaking research, which supports the thesis that religion contributes towards helping young people negotiate the passage from childhood to adulthood. Research also concludes that young people with religious affiliation may be more open to volunteering and participating in social outreach experiences. The American Journal of Epidemiology can be accessed online, and in its 10 September 2018 edition there is an account of its findings. A press release from the Harvard T.H. Chan School of Public Health, on 13 September 2018, reports that 'Participating in spiritual practices during childhood and adolescence may be a protective factor for a range of health and well-being outcomes in early childhood, according to a new study … Researchers found that people who attended weekly religious services or practiced daily prayer or meditation in their youth reported greater life satisfaction and positivity in their 20s.'[109] The report's author, Ying Chen, said, 'These findings are important for both our understanding of health and our understanding of parenting practices … Many children are raised religiously, and our study shows that this can powerfully affect their health behaviours, mental health, and overall happiness and well-being.'[110]

Psychologist Maureen Gaffney asserts that 'Being religious is associated with being happier, especially when this is expressed in actual religious behaviours, such as attending church services.'[111] However, she also suggests that 'this effect is less marked in European countries than in the USA'.[112] Even with that proviso, she concludes that 'Being religious makes people happier for many reasons,'[113] such as supporting people to find meaning in life, and especially during times of crisis. 'It also offers a collective identity and a reliable social network of like-minded people who share similar attitudes and values.'[114]

109. https://www.hsph.harvard.edu/news/press-releases/religious-upbringing-adult-health/
110. Ibid.
111. Maureen Gaffney, *Flourishing*, London: Penguin Random House UK, 2011, p. 123.
112. Ibid.
113. Ibid., p. 124.
114. Ibid.

This was also confirmed in a presentation to teachers in a Jesuit comprehensive school when psychologist Shane Martin 'spoke about six ways of being that keep people well, and one of the six was faith/prayer'. He elaborated by adding that 'I am not getting all holy now, I am just stating the fact that those who had prayer/faith as a regular part of their lives were more resilient and did better in terms of being able to cope and bounce back.'[115] This was one of the six steps he spoke about that support people's capacity to be resilient. With regard to the importance of religion, Abraham Heschel remarks that we 'teach the children how to measure, how to weigh. We fail to teach them how to revere, how to sense wonder and awe.'[116] As we saw in an earlier chapter, if wonder is extinguished, openness to other dimensions of life is also extinguished. A lack of openness to the transcendent undermines the creation of a hope-filled world. Heschel also makes the point that the Greeks learned in order to understand, the Jews learned in order to revere, and now we learn in order to exploit our common home, because 'the world is now a gigantic toolbox for the satisfaction' of needs.[117] The ideal aspiration is a combination of the Greek and the Jewish views, which are incorporated into Christianity, with faith trying to understand itself.

It can reasonably be argued that there are many good reasons for being religious, one of which, as already highlighted, is that it helps people to make meaning out of life, which gives a solid sense of direction and purpose as well as helping to deal with life's tragedies. Another reason is the community support which a private spirituality may lack. However, it seems that there is a convincing consensus to suggest that religion is, on balance, good for us as long as it steers clear of its more fanatical, violent, fundamentalist and literal expressions, all of which undermine its integrity and are a clear sign it's not from God. Pope Francis affirmed this viewpoint during his visit to Kazakhstan when he declared that 'harsh and repressive forms of religion belong not to the future but to the past'.[118] This also includes Christianity, which needs to be reimagined

115. Alan Hilliard (ed.), op. cit., p.130.
116. Abraham Joshua Heschel, op. cit., p. 36.
117. Ibid., p. 34.
118. 'Apostolic Journey of His Holiness Pope Francis to Kazakhstan', 15 September 2022, https://www.vatican.va/content/francesco/en/speeches/2022/september/documents/20220915-kazakhstan-finecongresso.html.

continually. The misguided harsh repressiveness of former times is a cause for shame and repentance.

If religion, keeping the memory of God alive, is so good for us, it's time to reconsider the role of religion in our lives and not be ashamed of it. It's time to learn from the sins of the past and move forward. Religion is another support to orient young people in the creation of a hope-filled world. 'Young people are messengers of peace and unity, in the present and in the future. It is they, more than anyone else, who call for peace and respect for the common home of creation.'[119] Ignatius would want us to engage any means that would be helpful in supporting our young people. If we can let go of our religious prejudices and start again by reimagining religion in a new dress, young people could inherit a legacy of hope-filled religion. As it finds its way forward religion needs to be in conversation with the culture, human experience and the scientific community. When a decision is tainted with prejudice or anger, it's not a good decision, because it's dishonest and unfaithful to who we are. It's easy to become a slave to prejudice or anger and remain in that deceptive comfort zone. It takes humility and honesty to name our prejudices and angers, but a person who wants to own their humanity will take on the challenge and move beyond a tabloid view of the world.

One of the contributors to the fracture and breakdown of society in many parts of the world is that the religious lodestar has become obscured. However, it also needs to be acknowledged that distorted views of religion have also done more harm than good, especially when religion is hijacked to support dehumanising ideologies. Without a responsible sense of purpose, direction and self-identity, we lose our way. The evidence is overwhelming as we hear regular news of violence, destruction and war on daily news broadcasts. Misinformation, fake news and unquestioned assumptions undermine trust and communication and serve to reinforce divisions. There is a malaise in society at large which is symptomatic of a deeper disorder rooted in our rejection of our identity as persons-in-relationship. We are our brothers' and sisters' keepers. Our flesh and blood incorporate us into the human family. We fool ourselves if we believe we

119. 'Apostolic Journey of His Holiness change to: Pope Francis to Kazakhstan', 15 September 2022, https://www.vatican.va/content/francesco/en/speeches/2022/september/documents/20220915-kazakhstan-finecongresso.html.

know with certainty all there is to be known. We don't experience life without employing our senses. Therefore, we conclude, without compelling evidence, that there is nothing beyond them. The narrative of Adam and Eve highlights that sin and death, alienation and dehumanisation entered our world through a failure to recognise and embrace the reality of who we are, persons-in relationship living in graced dependence. Rejection of that essential fact of life is the root of all evil. Thankfully, hope-filled luminaries from all walks of life, at home in their identity, often come to the rescue to break the cycle of pain and misery inspired by a 'hope for a great sea-change / On the far side of revenge. / Believe that a further shore / Is reachable from here. / Believe in miracles / And cures and healing wells.'[120] They respond to the call to arms in the knowledge that being men and women for and with others will advance God's plan for a wounded world, through the grace of God, by being faithful to who we are. We need to honestly answer the question, 'Who do you think you are?'

Hope is not lost. Altruistic and creative people of all ages, especially those with their lives ahead of them, will be the architects of a hope-filled world, rejecting the unexamined assumptions of the past. They will imagine possibilities and make them happen. It's up to us to support them as they model what a hope-filled future might look like. The future is in the hands of young people, given to us as a blessing from God to be ambassadors of hope. 'How has Christianity changed your life?' If we haven't tried it, we'll never know.

Questions	Ignatius answers
What's my life about?	I'm the image of God, trekking with others to God's house, doing what God does.
How do I make the journey?	I remember that I'm in solidarity with others in graced dependence.

120. Seamus Heaney, from 'The Cure at Troy', op. cit.

What does a hope-filled world look like?	We're sitting at the banquet of life where no one is excluded. All are welcome. The weapons are left outside.
Four faith preferences	Reflection, social/climate justice, hope for young people

Bibliography

Abbott, Walter, *The Documents of Vatican II*, New York, NY: The America Press, 1966.

Anonymous, Trans. Philip Boehm, *A Woman in Berlin*, London: Virago, 2005.

Alter, Robert, *The Art of Biblical Narrative*, Amazon Kindle, 26 April 2011.

Boyle, Gregory, *Tattoos on the Heart*, New York, NY: Free Press, 2011.

Carpini, John Delli, *Poetry as Prayer – Emily Dickinson*, Boston, MA: Pauline Books and Media, 2002.

Congregation for Catholic Education, *The Identity of a Catholic School for a Culture of Dialogue*, Vatican City, 2022.

Congregation for Catholic Education, *Educating Today and Tomorrow: A Renewing Passion (Instrumentum Laboris)*, Vatican City, 2014.

Day, Dorothy, *Loaves and Fishes: The inspiring story of the Catholic Worker Movement*, New York, NY: Harper and Row, 1963.

—*The Long Loneliness*, New York, NY: HarperOne, 2017.

Durcan, Paul, *The Art of Life*, London: Random House UK, 2004.

Edwards, Cliff, *Van Gogh and God: A Creative Spiritual Quest*, Chicago, IL: Loyola University Press, 1989.

Egan, Harvey D., *Karl Rahner: Mystic of Everyday Life*, New York, NY: The Crossroad Publishing Company, 1998.

Gaffney, Maureen, *Flourishing*, London: Penguin Random House UK, 2011.

Han, Byung-Chul and Steuer, Daniel, *The Disappearance of Rituals: A Topology of the Present*, Cambridge: Polity Press, 2020.

Healy, Mary, *The Gospel of Mark*, Ada, MI: Baker Academic, 2008.

Heaney, Seamus, *100 Poems*, London: Faber & Faber, 2018.

Heschel, Abraham Joshua, *God in Search of Man: A Philosophy of Judaism*, New York, NY: Farrar, Strauss & Giroux, 1976.

Hilliard, Alan (ed.), *Chaplains: Ministers of Hope*, Dublin: Messenger Publications, 2021.

Jesuit Apostolic Preferences, https://www.jesuits.global/uap/

Jesuit Schools: A Living Tradition in the 21st Century, Rome: Jesuit Education Commission, September 2019.

Jones, W. Paul, *Remnant Christianity in a Post-Christian World*, Eugene, OR: Wipf and Stock, 2021.

Kaminsky, Ilya, and Towler, Katherine, *A God in the House: Poets Talk About Faith*, North Adams, MA: Tupelo Press, 2014.

Kavanagh, Peter (ed.), *Patrick Kavanagh: The Complete Poems, arranged and edited by Peter Kavanagh*, Newbridge, The Goldsmith Press, 1988.

Keane, John B., *Sive*, Cork: Mercier Press, 2009 (first published 1959).

Larkin, Philip, *High Windows*, London: Faber & Faber, 2015.

Loewe, William P., *Introduction to Christology*, Collegeville, MN: The Liturgical Press, 1996.

Maher, Jim, SJ, *Pathways To A Decision*, Dublin: Messenger Publications, 2020.

McVerry, Peter, SJ, *The Meaning is in the Shadows*, Dublin: Veritas Publications, 2003.

Meissner, W. W., *Ignatius of Loyola: The Psychology of a Saint*, New Haven, CT: Yale University Press, 1992.

Morley, Janet, *The Heart's Time*, London: SPCK, 2011.

Oakley, Mark, *The Collage of God*, London: Darton, Longman and Todd, 2001.

O'Collins, Gerald, *Interpreting Jesus*, London: Mowbray, 1992.

O'Driscoll, Denis, *Exemplary Damages*, London: Anvil Press Poetry, 2002.

Orr, Gregory, *The Blessing: A Memoir*, Tulsa, OK: Council Oak Books, 2019.

Orwell, George, *Animal Farm*, London: Penguin Books, 1972 edition (first published 1945).

Pope Francis, *The Joy of the Gospel*, Dublin: Veritas Publications, 2013.

Pope Francis, *Laudato Si'* (On Care for Our Common Home), Dublin: Veritas Publications, 2015.

Parenti, Michael, *Power And The Powerless*, New York, NY: St Martin's Press, 1978.

— *The Culture Struggle*, New York, NY: Seven Stories Press, 2006.

— *Contrary Notions: The Michael Parenti Reader*, San Francisco, CA: City Lights Books, 2007.

— *Waiting For Yesterday: Pages from a Street Kid's Life*, New York, NY: Bordighera Press, 2013.

Phillips, Catherine, *Gerard Manley Hopkins*, Oxford: Oxford University Press, 1986.

Puhl, Louis J., SJ, *The Spiritual Exercises of St. Ignatius*, Chicago IL: Loyola University Press, 1952.

Saint-Exupéry, Antoine de, (trans. Katherine Woods) *The Little Prince*, London: William Heinemann, 1954. Reprinted London: Mammoth, 1991.

Smith, Maggie, *Good Bones*, North Adams, MA: Tupelo Press, 2017.

Untermeyer, Louis, *New Enlarged Anthology of Robert Frost's Poems*, New York, NY: Washington Square Press, 1971.

Williams, Niall, *This is Happiness*, London: Bloomsbury Publishing, 2019.

Yeats, W. B., *The Collected Poems of W.B. Yeats*, Wordsworth Poetry Library, 2000.

PATHWAYS
TO A
DECISION
WITH IGNATIUS OF LOYOLA

JIM MAHER SJ

Messenger (MJP) Publications

www.messenger.ie